Contents

List of figures, tables and boxes

Figures

Tables

Boxes

List of abbreviations

ARK	Absolute Return for Kids
ASDAN	Award Scheme Development and Accreditation Network
ATL	Association of Teachers and Lecturers
BitC	Business in the Community
BWP	Brooke Weston Partnership
CBI	Confederation of British Industry
CC	County Council
CfBT	Centre for British Teachers
CSR	corporate social responsibility
CTC	City Technology College
DCSF	Department of Children, Schools and Families
DfE	Department for Education
DfES	Department for Education and Skills
ECAC	Every Child a Chance
ECAR	Every Child a Reader
ECC	Every Child Counts
EET	Enterprise Education Trust
FC	Football Club
FCO	Foreign and Commonwealth Office
GDST	Girls Day Schools Trust
GWF	Garfield Weston Foundation
IoE	Institute of Education
IPPR	Institute for Public Policy Research
JA	Junior Achievement
KIPP	Knowledge is Power Program
LSE	London School of Economics and Political Science
NAHT	National Association of Head Teachers
NCSL	The National College for Leadership of Schools and Children's Services (formerly the National College for School Leadership)
NEET	(young people) not in education, employment or training
NESTA	National Endowment for Science, Technology and the Arts
NPC	New Philanthropy Capital
NSN	New Schools Network
NSPCC	National Society for the Prevention of Cruelty to Children
NUT	National Union of Teachers
Ofsted	Office for Standards in Education
PEF	Private Equity Foundation
QCA	Qualifications and Curriculum Authority

RSA	Royal Society of Arts
SHINE	Support and Help in Education
SIFE	Students in Free Enterprise
SSAT	Specialist Schools and Academies Trust
TES	*Times Educational Supplement*
TF	Teach First
TFA	Teach for America
UBS	Union Bank of Switzerland
ULT	United Learning Trust

About the authors

Stephen J. Ball is Karl Mannheim Professor of the Sociology of Education at the Institute of Education, University of London. His work is in 'policy sociology' and he has conducted a series of ESRC-funded studies which focus on issues of social class and policy. He has an honorary doctorate from Turku University, Finland, and is Visiting Professor at the University of San Andrés, Argentina and a Fellow of the British Academy.

Carolina Junemann is a researcher at the Institute of Education, University of London. She has a Bachelor's degree in Sociology from Universidad de Buenos Aires, Argentina, a Master's degree from Teachers College, Columbia University and a PhD in Education from the Institute of Education, University of London, where she currently researches issues of education policy in the UK.

Acknowledgements

This research would not have been possible without the cooperation of those people who agreed to be interviewed (see Appendix) and we are very grateful to them for their time. We also had considerable help from a number of personal assistants in setting up meetings. Paul Laluvein did a great job in transcribing the interviews accurately and quickly. Clare Thornbury kept a careful eye on our finances. A number of people were helpful in making comments on drafts of papers and presentations, including Colin Crouch, Helen Gunter, Martin Smith, Roger King, Mark Goodwin, Becky Francis and Lorna Unwin, and participants in British Educational Research Association (BERA) seminars.

ONE

Policy networks and new governance

The focus of this book is on ongoing and related changes in education policy, policy networks and governance in England; in particular, the increasing participation of philanthropy and business in policy and service delivery. In this chapter we will sketch out the conceptual terrain across which our analysis moves and introduce some of the key ideas that we draw upon and deploy later. However, this is neither an exhaustive review of the literatures on policy networks and network governance nor an attempt to engage in the arcane and internecine debates and struggles with which the governance research literature is riven. Rather, we will outline a position that we take up in relation to this literature and its disputes, as seems constructive to understanding what is currently going on in English education policy. Our focus is substantive and analytical. We are interested in exploring how educational governance is being done and by whom. We are interested in this as indicative and illustrative of what seem to be more general shifts and changes in governance methods and mechanisms. We also consider *some* of the effects and consequences of these changes, but that is not our primary purpose here. The book draws on research that was focused particularly on the roles of philanthropy and businesses in education policy,[1] and these have become increasingly significant and topical in current education and social policy. We will return to a discussion of some of the general issues of governance in the final chapter.

What to read first?

This chapter focuses on issues of governance theory and network method and their relationship. We begin by introducing the contrast and move between government and governance, which has been used extensively in recent political science to address changes in the form and modalities of the state, and we identify some key features of what is called network governance. This involves a discussion of some rather slippery, confusing and contested concepts. Specifically, we begin to explore the 'work' of network governance that is done in the social relations and exchanges within policy networks – those communities of social actors and organisations concerned with and engaged in policy conversations, policy influence and service delivery in the public sector. The second concern of this chapter is with the question of how to research these 'new' forms and relationships of governing. We outline an approach – network ethnography – based on a combination of social network analysis and qualitative research methods and consider some of the possibilities and limitations of this.

At this stage you may wish to skip the rest of this chapter and look at some of the examples and analysis work presented in the following chapters before coming back to the issues of theory and method.

From government to governance?

> Whether one points to the grand narratives of network society (Castells, 2000b) or reflexive modernity (Giddens, 1991) or the more concrete and specific accounts of the formation and functioning of networks of public agencies, private organisations and diverse groups and citizens (for example Rhodes, 1988), one finds the articulation of a need for rearticulating our understanding of government and authority based on an ontological change that has taken place in recent decades. (Triantafillou, 2004a, p 489)

> The hierarchical model of government is in decline, pushed by governments' appetites to solve ever more complicated problems and pulled by new tools that allow innovators to fashion creative responses. This push and pull is gradually producing a new government model, in which executives' core responsibilities no longer centre on managing people and programs but on organising resources – often belonging to others – to produce public value. We call this trend 'governing by network'. (Eggers, 2008)

Working with and on a set of empirical materials (see below), this book seeks both to add to a body of research within political science, sociology and social geography that is concerned with changes in the policy process and new methods of governing society, that is, with the shift from 'the government of a unitary state to governance in and by networks' (Bevir and Rhodes, 2003, p 41), and to make a modest contribution to the conceptualisation of policy networks and governance. The analysis of policy networks is sometimes called the 'Anglo-governance model' and the most prominent and influential figure in the field is Rod Rhodes (see Marsh and Rhodes, 1992; Rhodes, 1995; Rhodes, 1997; Marinetto, 2005), although there are also a lively US school of public network management research (see Agranoff and Maguire, 2001) and a set of German groups working on inter-organisational theory (Marin and Mayntz, 1991; Börzel, 1997; Scharpf, 1997) and there have been significant recent contributions from the Dutch public management school (Kickert et al, 1997; Kooiman, 2003). Across all of these literatures a contrast is drawn between *governance*, which is accomplished through the 'informal authority' of diverse and flexible networks, and *government*, which is carried out through hierarchies or specifically within administrations and by bureaucratic methods. Policy networks are presented as both a real change in the structure of the polity and an emergent and distinct form of governance and a move beyond the methods of New Public Management (see below) – a 'reassembly', as Clarke and Newman (2009) describe it. That is, network governance is a further move 'beyond the public bureaucracy state' (Hood, 1990) and a further 'reinventing of government' (Osborne and Gaebler, 1992) – a new kind of governing mechanism that relies 'on a dense fabric of lasting ties and networks that provide key resources of expertise, reputation and legitimization' (Grabher, 2004, p 104).

Rhodes (1981, 1988), who has made the terminology of policy networks popular in the British context, was influenced by the continental European literature on intergovernmental relationships, with its emphasis on the structural relationships between political institutions based on patterns of resource-dependency as the crucial element in policy networks. The model initially developed by Marsh and Rhodes (1992), besides downplaying the role of agency, argues that network structures can define the agenda and outcomes of a policy network. The types of network membership and the distribution of resources among members lead to the definition of different types of policy networks, ranging from policy communities (tight policy networks) to issue networks (loose policy networks) (see below). Rhodes (1995, p 9) uses 'the term network to describe the several interdependent actors involved in delivering services ... these networks are made up of organizations which need to exchange resources (money, information, expertise) to achieve their objectives'.

Slippage, policy networks/network governance

Our emphasis is primarily on the actors and interactions within and across networks, and the 'work' or networking of participating organisations, rather than on network structures and the distribution of resources, although, as Smith (2000) puts it, 'A dynamic interplay exists between the network structure and the agents within it.' We use policy network theory as a lens through which to examine network governance, with a particular focus on the interactions between actors and groups within education policy-making fields and their influence on the policy process.[2] As part of this we do seek to identify some of the 'resources' that different sorts of actors bring into play to achieve their ends. Here we use network as a method, a means for tracing and representing social relations within the field of policy, and as an analytic tool. Nonetheless, we are also attracted by Triantafillou's (2004a, p 489) approach to network governance as a form of governmentality and 'as a specific form of rule that governs at a distance through norms of efficiency, agency and accountability'. He suggests that governance networks bring into play particular kinds of expert knowledge, ranging from industrial psychology to auditing, which 'inform, enframe and enable particular ways of intervening' (Triantafillou, 2004b, p 14), shape the definition of social problems and set standards for efficiency, accountability and participation in the political process. He also argues that the autonomies and de-concentrations of network governance promote self-steering, responsibility and collaboration as disciplinary techniques (we will return to this in the final chapter). However, we are going to be unashamedly promiscuous in relation to the materials and approaches upon which we draw to describe and discuss the English education policy networks that are our focus. Our intention is to move between data and theory in order to adumbrate some substantive findings and offer some conceptual elaborations and to indicate some possibilities for further analysis.

Despite the massive recent interest in these issues, it is also necessary to maintain some scepticism in relation to governance and policy networks. Stoker (2004, p 439) offers a caution to anyone tempted by the attractions of the governance literature, which he likens, in a review of Kooiman's (2003) book, to Tolkien's *The Fellowship of the Ring*: 'It offers a world of governance comprehensively specified and described into which student and researcher can step.' The danger is both that governing is understood and analysed in terms of what may be new and different without attending adequately to what has remained the same and that developments that do not 'fit' the world according to governance are downplayed or ignored. The term 'new' is used often in this book, sometimes quoting others, sometimes by ourselves, and we are always in danger of neglecting that which has not changed. The authors quoted at the beginning of the chapter are in no doubt about the 'reality' of and extent of the changes involved. The problem here will be to attempt to describe and conceptualise what has changed and what has stayed the same in current forms and modes of governing. Our point will be that there is no absolute change here, but rather, a shift in the balance or mix between the different elements of government – bureaucracies, markets and networks.

Much of the literature on the conceptualisation and description of network governance is concerned with its structures rather than its *hows* and *whys*. Despite the incredible bulk of the writing on network governance and policy networks, Provan and Kenis (2008, p 229) point out that 'there is still a considerable discrepancy between the acclamation and attention networks receive and the knowledge we have about the overall functioning of networks'. In part, this discrepancy stems from a failure of comparison and accumulation: there are many studies of the work of policy networks in different settings at different levels, but these studies have not been consolidated or used to systematically interrogate the theory of network governance. This book seeks to describe and conceptualise a particular set of policy networks, but it is also about the *how* of governance: in the field of education policy, how do these networks function? It also makes some attempts to address the why question: why are the developments described happening, and why now? We return to the question of the robustness of governance theory in the final chapter.

Let us return to the problem of definition. *Network governance*, although the term is used somewhat loosely and diversely 'to refer to a bewildering array of different phenomena and governmental practices' (Triantafillou, 2004b, p 2) essentially involves the treatment of seemingly intractable public policy issues – 'wicked social problems' that 'defy efforts to delineate their boundaries and to identify their causes' (Rittel and Webber, 1973, p 167, in Williams, 2002, p 104) – through forms of managerial and organisational response 'around collaboration, partnership and networking' (Williams, 2002). 'Wicked' social problems are interrelated and complex, thus difficult to understand and even more difficult to respond to, especially if responses are limited to traditional solutions that have failed before. 'Wicked' problems typically involve many stakeholders with different values and problems and have long histories and tangled origins and causes. Network governance, it is suggested, brings new solutions to bear upon such problems by 'catalyzing all sectors – public, private and voluntary – into action' (Osborne and Gaebler, 1992). Governments are redefining themselves 'as facilitators engaged in value chains, and working through markets rather than acting as autarkic doers who owned, operated and produced everything themselves' (Wanna, 2009, p 266). This is a shared problem-solving process, or what Wanna calls 'co-labouring'. It is argued by the advocates of network governance that this brings a greater degree of flexibility and adjustment to the complexity of existing conditions. Eggers (2008, p 23) argues: 'The traditional, hierarchical government model simply does not meet the demands of this complex, rapidly changing age. Rigid bureaucratic systems with command-and-control procedures, narrow work restrictions and inward-looking cultures and operational models are particularly ill suited to addressing problems that often transcend organisational boundaries.' Newman (2001, p 108) elaborates, pointing out that the governance literature views networks 'in terms of plural actors engaged in a reflexive process of dialogue and information exchange', or as Agranoff (2003, p 28) puts it, 'networks provide venues for collaborative solutions' and 'mobilise innovations'. In slightly stronger terms, Rhodes argues that network governance 'refers to self-organising, inter-organizational networks characterized by interdependence, resource-exchange, rules of the game, and significant autonomy from the state' (Rhodes, 1997, p 15). Through all of this, more and more public services provision is being delivered through a mix of 'strategic alliances, joint working arrangements, networks, partnerships and many other forms of collaboration across sectoral and organizational boundaries' (Williams, 2002, p 103), based upon 'relations involving mutuality and interdependence as opposed to hierarchy and independence' (Peterson, 2003, p 1). Nonetheless, a number of commentators point out that these interdependencies are 'asymmetric' (see Rhodes, 1997). The argument is that these network-based forms of coordination, are displacing both hierarchy and markets as the dominant mode of interaction within public services and policy (Kooiman, 1993; Rhodes, 1997; Pierre, 2000; Pierre and Peters, 2000).[3] In general terms this is the move towards a 'polycentric state' and 'a shift in the centre of gravity around which policy cycles move' (Jessop, 1998 p 32), although many of the accounts of network governance omit entirely or deal only in passing with the role of the private sector in these movements and interdependences. Other writers argue that network governance and policy networks can provide an environment for consensus building and therefore limit the emergence of implementation resistance (Marin and Mayntz, 1991). As Besussi (2006, p 18) puts it 'the promise of policy networks and of the mode of governance they represent is to produce more effective and legitimate policies, without resting upon the authority and limitations of a single representative political body'. Koppenjan and Klijn (2004, p 25) cut through this definitional undergrowth with a simple rendition which is apposite and useful as far as our project here is concerned. They say: 'In the world of network governance, government is understood to be located alongside business and civil society actors in a complex game of public policy formation, decision-making and implementation' (Koppenjan and Klijn, 2004, p 25).

Some versions of network governance also relate the changes adumbrated above to a move to more democratic forms of governance (Sørensen and Torfing, 2008), while other writers suggest that network governance creates a 'democratic deficit' as the processes of policy and governance become more dispersed and more opaque (March and Olsen, 1989). That is, it is argued, not only do policy networks blur the boundaries between state and society but they also expose the policy-making process to particularistic power games. The 'territory of influence' (Mackenzie and Lucio, 2005) over policy is expanded, but at the same time the spaces of policy are diversified and dissociated. As a result, as these new sites within the contexts of policy influence and text production (Ball, 1994) proliferate, there is a concomitant increase in the opacity of policy making. Within the functioning of policy networks it is unclear what may have been said to whom, where, with what effect and in exchange for what (see Cohen, 2004). As Skelcher (1998) argues, these new social and political relationships of policy are also part of and contribute to other related features of the changing state – what he calls 'the appointed state' and what he also (Skelcher, 2000) describes as the 'congested state'. Between them, these descriptors seek to capture both the proliferation and fragmented array of agencies and actors involved in local and regional governance and in the provision of public services (Sullivan and Skelcher, 2004), and to give some indication of the 'democratic deficit' that results from the increasing participation of quangos and other non-elected agencies and businesses and voluntary organisations in the governance of 'public' institutions and their 'weaker accountability, audit and governance standards' (Skelcher, 1998, p 181). Similarly, Keast, Mandell and Brown (2006, p 27) argue that 'This situation leads to governance complexity and what is contended to be a "crowded" policy domain in which differing governance arrangements, policy prescriptions, participants and processes bump up against and even compete with each other to cause overlap and confusion'.

In all of this, Shamir (2008, p 6) argues, 'governments relinquish some of their privileged authoritative positions'. However, in thinking about and looking at the work of network governance it is important that we do not underestimate the continuing effectivity of the powers of the state, but also important that we do not in abstract overestimate them, nor treat the state as an undifferentiated whole. The move to the use of forms of network governance in some areas of state activity may involve a loss of power in some parts of the state, at the same time as there are gains in other parts. If the gains are bigger than the losses (to use power very crudely), then the state may overall have greater powers than before. In the exercise of network governance the state is also acquiring new powers and forms of power, as Triantafillou suggests – that is, a form of 'metagovernance' (Jessop, 2002, p 242), control over the 'conditions of governing'. This is where the concept of governmentality is relevant and useful in understanding how new policy technologies, like performativity, work to produce new governance subjects, inviting and inciting us to make ourselves more effective, to work on ourselves to improve our productivity and to feel guilty or inadequate if we do not (Ball, 2003). However, in many respects the shift to polycentrism and interdependence also involves forms of experimentation and ad hocery (see Parker, 2007) on the part of the state. Network governance is not a new stable structure for managing state and society, it is made up of a set of more or less unstable methods and relationships which, if they do not work as expected, can be dispensed with and replaced. There is no ruptural change, but rather, small moves and changes that accumulate overtime, with occasional instances of back-tracking.

The UK, and England in particular, is taken by most commentators to be an 'implementer' and 'benchmark model' of both New Public Management and network governance. Skelcher (2007, p 26) argues that England is a useful and interesting case and:

> can be considered the outlier in terms of reforms of public governance and management. A continual process of experimentation since the 1980s has significantly changed the institutions of local policy deliberation and delivery, giving a much stronger emphasis to interactive decision-making by networks of governmental, civil society and business actors, structured around 'partnerships' – new collaborative spaces for the local governance of specific policy sectors and communities. The English case enables the predominant view on governance networks to be refined and contextualised. It helps to clarify and accentuate

particular features, and to relate these to the ways in which
the governance of England has developed in recent decades.

It is certainly the case, as we hope to demonstrate, that in England
education and social policy are now being 'thought', influenced and
done, locally and nationally, in many different sites by an increasing
number and diverse set of actors and organisations. The education
policy community is increasingly heterogeneous (see Ball, 2008b), and
network governance within it is highly developed and is developing
further, and has been fostered both by New Labour and the 2010
Coalition government. We outline the English case of education
network governance in the next chapter.

Networks and communities

As indicated already, there is a degree of misleading clarity about
the concept of networks, as used in the governance literature. It is
either used very abstractly to describe general changes in the form of
government or deployed to refer to a very wide variety of real and
practical social relationships. Furthermore, some of the writing on
networks is normative (as noted above) and the distinction between
prescription and analysis is sometimes blurred. The idea of policy
networks as we use it here is a descriptive and analytic term that refers
to a form of governance that interweaves and interrelates markets and
hierarchies – a kind of messy hinterland that supplements and sometimes
subverts these other forms. The vagaries of the term are avoided, as far
as possible, by focusing on a set of specific network relations and on
a highly interlinked 'policy community' that 'catalyses' philanthropy
and business in the delivery of education services and reconfigures
and disseminates a particular set of education policy discourses. The
term 'policy community' also presents some difficulties, but such
communities, as noted above, can be thought of on a continuum of
social and ideological cohesion. 'At one end of this continuum are
policy communities, as integrated, stable and exclusive policy networks;
at the other end are issue networks of loosely connected, multiple, and
often conflict-ridden members' (Skogstad, 2005, p 5). The examples
examined in this account are closer to the former than the latter, but
are not as integrated, stable and exclusive as all that. Newman (2001,
p 108) offers the important caution that 'Networks are informal and
fluid, with shifting membership and ambiguous relationships and
accountabilities'; again, that is the case in some of our examples, but not
all. Nonetheless, the community to which we refer is institutionalised

and stabilised via the work of various nodal actors (see below) and lead organisations (for example Specialist Schools and Academies Trust (SSAT), Private Equity Foundation (PEF), New Schools Network and Teach First). It also consists of 'personal relationships within a shared framework' (Marsh and Rhodes, 1992, p 17) and has its own 'internal relationships of trust and deference' (McPherson and Raab, 1988, p 405). Increasingly, it would appear, it is in 'these decentralized, and more or less regularized and coordinated, interactions between state and societal actors that policy making unfolds' (Coleman and Skogstad, 1990, p 4). Wright-Mills calls this, a new form of 'institutional mechanics' (Wright-Mills, 1959, p 20). Indeed, by 'examining networks we are looking at the institutionalization of power relations' (Marsh and Smith, 2000, p 6). *However, to reiterate, such influences and relationships are of course not entirely new; it is their extent, specificity, directness and degree of integration with government and state organisations that is different* – as we hope to demonstrate. That is to say, the many actors and organisations referred to below are now heavily engaged in various mundane and informal ways in the day-to-day business of the state through face-to-face meetings, discussions, representations and consultations. They bring particular sorts of perspectives, methods and interests to bear on and in the policy process. People move across and within such communities, and there are new kinds of policy and governance careers that can be constructed within them. However, the nature of the relations between members (as represented by the arrows in the network diagrams that are deployed in the later chapters) is not the same in every case (see below on network ethnography). Indeed, the networks we present are partial in themselves; by definition there are limits both to what can be known about them and how they work and what can be or should be included (before density overwhelms perception and understanding); and they are also partial in that they are interconnected into a broader framework of governance, which is also difficult to 'represent' visually. This also means that the boundaries of these networks are often difficult to discern and, in the cases presented, the limits of connectivity are often pragmatic and reflect more the limitations of data collection and problems of representation (see below) rather than any firm cut-off points in the social relations between actors. Of course not all participations are equally significant or influential within policy networks, some people (or organisations) who occupy multiple positions and who are adept in the arts of networking act as nodes; they join things up and 'span boundaries' (see Chapter Four). In doing so they accumulate valuable information and move ideas and influences between sectors. Location in a network is key to social capital, for example for those who link across 'structural holes' (Burt, 2001). Networks are made up of relationships in which social capital can be deployed, invested and accumulated. Lin (2002) also considers that the resources that actors bring to a network increase the social capital of the network – this is certainly evident in some of the examples discussed later.

Participations are also multifaceted: individual actors may be involved in networks in a variety of different ways: for example sponsorship, contracting, advice, committee membership, and so on. Contacts and links also vary in their significance. The forms of exchange involved are often unclear or multifaceted. One of the interpretive problems involved in thinking about how these networks work is that of deciding, at least in the case of some participants, where business ends and philanthropy or public service begins and to what extent philanthropy is a means of influence or a form of 'identity-work' (Breeze, 2007) or both. These communities establish productive and potentially profitable relationships within the state for non-state actors, they provide access to valuable insider knowledge (see Ball, 2007) and enhance public and personal esteem (see Chapter Four). Participation can lead to the receipt of awards, honours, appointments and positions in and around the state itself; interests are served and rewards achieved. However, perhaps it is pointless to attempt to pin down precisely the motives involved here or to try to separate out different elements, and better to accept that motives for participation and the outcomes of participation are contradictory and mixed. 'Giving' or participation in policy events is also a way of registering a presence and making 'purposeful' relationships with contractors and opinion makers and demonstrating a public service commitment (see Ball, 2007).

The networks contain flows of ideas as well as flows of people, and ideas are carried back and forth across the boundaries between the public and private sectors. These are discursive or epistemic communities. Through social relationships trust is established and particular views and discourses are legitimated. They structure, constrain and enable the circulation of ideas and give 'institutional force' to policy utterances, ensuring what can count as 'sensible' policy and limiting the possibilities of policy. As Richards and Smith (2002, p 207) note, networks 'simplify the policy process by limiting actions, problems and solutions' and new policy narratives are articulated and validated with them (see Ball, 2007). Indeed these networks both are carriers of discourse and contain key sites of discourse, wherein new policy ideas are naturalised and made eminently thinkable and obvious as the constituents of public sector reform. Specifically in this case the 'enterprise narrative' (see Students in Free Enterprise [SIFE], National Foundation for Teaching

Enterprise and The Academy for Enterprise – Chapter Three). This is a new hegemonic vision of governance and social relations generally, which inserts competition and entrepreneurialism into the heart of the project of state education. Such narratives in turn serve to repopulate the field of policy, legitimating new actors. That is, particular versions of reform serve to enroll and give voice to new participants; they also rework the possibilities of public sector delivery and establish new key ideas and new social logics. These new actors can also be thought of, in Jessop's terms, as the bearers of a new accumulation strategy and he notes their 'increasing participation ... in shaping education mission statements' (Jessop, 2002, p 167).

In more general terms network theory and methods are set within a broad set of epistemological and ontological shifts across political science, sociology and social geography that involve a lessening of interest in social structures and an increasing emphasis on flows and mobilities (of people, capital and ideas, for example 'policies in motion' (Peck, 2003)). This is what Urry (2003, p 157) calls the 'mobility turn', that is, a focus on the 'spatialising' of social relations, on travel and other forms of movement and other transnational interactions and forms of sociality. All of this is of course attendant upon the overwhelming interest in recent years in the processes of 'globalisation'. The focus on *mobilities* takes into account large-scale economic and political changes, on the one hand, and cultural changes and changes in identity and subjectivity on the other,[4] and what Larner (2003, p 511) calls the 'apparently mundane practices' through which the global is produced. *The network* is a key trope and analytic device within this refocusing of attention as a kind of connective tissue that joins up and provides *some* durability to these distant and fleeting forms of social interaction – 'circulatory systems that connect and interpenetrate' the local (Peck, 2003, p 229). As Urry (2003, p 170) puts it very simply: 'Social life at least for many in the "west" and "north" is increasingly networked.' Policy networks are one kind of this new 'social', involving particular kinds of social relationships, subjectivities and identities, flows and movements in and beyond the nation-state. As noted already, they constitute new kinds of policy communities, usually based upon shared conceptions of social problems and their solutions, although they sometimes contain 'strange bedfellows' (as we shall see).

Network ethnography: the research

The research upon which we draw here has involved three sets of activities: extensive and exhaustive internet searches around particular edu-businesses, (corporate) philanthropies, philanthropists and philanthropically funded programmes;[5] interviews with some key edu-business people, and 'new' philanthropists and philanthropic foundations interested and involved in education (and attendance at some related meetings and events) (see Appendix); and the use of these searches and interviews to construct 'policy networks'. Together these constitute something that might be called a 'method' of 'network ethnography' (Wright-Mills, 1959, p 20). That is, a mapping of the form and content of policy relations in a particular field, a variation of what Bevir and Rhodes (2003) present as 'ethnographic analyses of governance in action' – but in their case not one that allows for much in the way of 'thick description' and one that perversely 'denies' context. Howard (2002, p 550) makes the point that 'Whereas social network analysis renders an overarching sketch of interaction, it will fail to capture detail on incommensurate yet meaningful relationships'. Network ethnography aims to go some way in remedying this failure. Nonetheless, this is not simply the application of familiar methods to new data; the focus here is on a particular form of relationships and interactions and power that should not be made too familiar, too quickly. The techniques and approaches being deployed here are being 'tried and tested' and will need further elaboration and development. We do not claim or aim for any completeness of account 'but rather to channel attention' (Riles, 2000, p 20) to new phenomena, and indeed we have avoided giving too much attention to network-mapping technologies.

Our method of 'network ethnography' leans, as the name suggests, towards the anthropological version of network analysis (Knox et al, 2006), with an emphasis on the understanding of the contents, transactions and meanings (see McCormick et al, 2011). Meaning within network relations, according to Castells (2000a, p 7), is 'the symbolic identification by an actor of the purpose of his/her/their action', and he goes on to say: 'The consolidation of shared meaning through crystallization of practices in socio-temporal configurations creates cultures, that is systems of values and beliefs ...', that is, policy communities. Even so, within such communities there are core and peripheral members, those who are stable and others who are transient, held together by intricate interdependencies; social networks 'involve a variety of social and communicative logics, different time scales and various modes of interaction' (Grabher, 2004, p 106). We tend to see network structure as flowing from transactions rather than vice versa and focus on networks themselves as 'object and subject of enquiry and attention' (Knox et al, 2006, p 128). Projects, interests and commitments of different kinds are clustered in the networks, which are reconfigured over time and in relation to new tasks and opportunities, and in many cases expand and take on new roles. Thus, network 'evolution' is important (Provan and Kenis, 2008), but mostly unattended to in research, as is the question of 'how they get started in the first place' (p 20). We will try to say something at least about both of these issues, but Provan and Kenis (2008) assert that 'systematic research on network evolution is needed' (p 20). We are also very cognisant of the point made by Savage and Williams (2008, p 6) that 'To be effective, network connections need to be linked to other lines of analysis'. This field of study also, indirectly at least, makes a contribution to the study of elites and what Savage and Williams (2008) call 'remembering elites' and particularly 'the importance of financialization in remembering elites' (p 12). Nonetheless, alongside meaning we are also interested in the pattern of ties and structure – clustering, nodes, boundary spanners, asymmetry, density and connectivity, and so on and we comment on or explore some of these features of the networks we address in later chapters. It would have been possible to have subjected our networks to more systematic structural analysis, but we chose to concentrate our efforts and attention on meanings and transactions and to respond to Dicken et al (2001, p 93) asserting that the task of network methodology 'must be to identify the actors in these networks, their power and capacities, and the ways through which they exercise their power through association within networks of relationships'.

Network analysis and network governance

Let us say a little more about social network analysis and policy networks. As noted already, there is a degree of misleading clarity about the concept of networks, particularly as used in the governance literature. It is either used very abstractly to describe general changes in the form of government or modalities of the state, or deployed to refer to a very wide variety of real and practical social relationships. Indeed, Besussi (2006, p 1) suggests that 'nowhere is to be found a common understanding of what policy networks are and how they operate. Little agreement exists even on whether policy networks are to be considered as a metaphor, a method or a proper theory with explanatory power.' In what follows *network* is deployed in different but related ways. As explained above, it is a method, a technique for looking at, thinking about and representing the structure of policy communities and their social relationships. It works to capture and describe *some aspects* of these relationships, or more precisely some of the more *visible* aspects of these relationships. Network is both an analytic and explanatory device in this account – it is a tool for describing how things actually are 'out there', or at least how they are changing; it is an object of study as well as a method. It is used to represent a set of 'real' changes in the forms and methods of governance of education, both nationally and globally. These changing forms and methods of governance are one dimension of what Castells (2000a, p 7) calls 'network society' that are 'constantly produced and reproduced through symbolic interaction between actors framed by … social structure and at the same time acting to change or reproduce it'.

Finally, the use of network as an analytic device for researching and describing and visualising governance relationships has many problems. Some of these problems have been well rehearsed in the social network analysis literature (for example, McCormick et al, 2011) but we want to draw attention to some that are relevant here. One very basic issue raised by Goodwin (2009) is whether the use of the device actually constructs the outcome, that is, 'if you look for networks you will find them'. There is some truth to that, but the response is to be able to demonstrate the effects of work that networks do in terms of policy processes and governance. That having been said, the distribution of power and capabilities within policy networks is not easy to 'measure' or represent. It is very difficult to map empirically 'the structured relationships of power' (Goodwin, 2009, p 682) within policy networks. How do we access and then 'measure' or calculate differential resources and capabilities embedded within the asymmetries of power relations? How do we relate these to the use of power and the different interests and goals of participants? A focus on specific events or crises may be one way forward. We believe that there are no existing research methods for addressing these tasks. Among other difficulties, almost by definition, as noted already, network relations are opaque, consisting in good part of informal social exchanges, negotiations and compromises that go on 'behind the scenes' or are done virtually. How are these to be mapped and characterised? Social media like Twitter, Facebook and blogs are new and underused sources of data that are relevant here. There are also concomitant conceptual and empirical problems arising from the (in)stability and short-term existence of some networks and network relations. Again almost by definition, network forms of governance are not fixed, and may contain some fleeting, fragile and experimental components. How do we capture changes in participation, capabilities and asymmetries over time? This also relates to the point noted above about network evolution. This is both an analytical and representational problem. The representational problem arises inasmuch that network diagrams are very inadequate and misleading devices for capturing and representing networks and network relations. They freeze movement and evolution and are always out of date.

Network diagrams are 'visualisations' of complex relationships, but they are also a distortion of these relationships. They have a particular and rather dull aesthetic, or rather, perhaps they suffer from what Riles (2000, p 19) calls an 'aesthetic failure' that she sees as endemic to the network form. They 'fix' a set of connections that are often in movement and 'flatten' what is an uneven and dispersed set of diverse relationships – both 'distant' or virtual and face-to-face. Networks contain both social actors and non-human actants, they consist of people, programmes, organisations, sites and events – people are 'in' these events and places, at different times, and move between them; as they do so they are 'doing' governing and policy and, indeed, 'doing globalisation'. The networks deployed here also vary in their structural patterns of relationships: some are 'tighter' than others. Looseness and tightness can be said to be captured simply by the degree of connectivity within a network, but may also be something to do with the nature or quality of the social relationships involved. This highlights again the epistemological differences between the structural and anthropological, quantitative and qualitative, approaches to network analysis.

Put most simply but most pointedly, the question is, both in the construction and representation of network diagrams – what do the arrows mean? What sorts of relationships and/or exchanges do they stand for? Are they equivalent? What is the strength of these relationships? What is the direction of flow? How do the relationships and their strengths change over time? Indeed, what counts as a network relationship and what should be discounted? There are some forms of quantitative analysis of social networks that seek to 'measure' networks in a literal sense – their degree of integration or interconnectedness, and their boundaries, the identification of nodes or hegemons or boundary spanners or holes. However, to a great extent there is a mismatch between what can be measured and what, from the point of view of policy sociology, is interesting and significant. We will address some of these problems in the various analyses that follow and we hope to point to some ways forward for the policy network method, but cannot promise simple or clear solutions.

The book is organised as follows: Chapter Two traces some of the developments and changes in forms of education governance in England, as these relate to the public sector, through New Labour into Coalition policy – from the 'Third Way' to the 'Big Society'. These are set within broader processes of public sector transformation, and the different aspects of transformation are related together in the example of the Garfield Weston Foundation. Chapter Three focuses on new philanthropy and the discourse of enterprise and looks at some of the contemporary entanglements of 'new' philanthropy with social and education policy by exploring the philanthropic involvements of Goldman Sachs, SHINE, the HSBC Global Education Trust and the Enterprise Education Trust. In Chapter Four we look at how networks work, concentrating on the actors and interactions within the networks. We focus on 'opportunities' for influence on the policy process, look at the work of boundary spanners and relate all of this through the examples of the KPMG Foundation and the Every Child a Chance Trust. Chapter Five focuses on some of the sorts of 'new', 'hybrid' actors involved in the processes of new governance (specifically ARK, Teach First and the New Schools Network). We look at their activities, perspectives and interests and discuss the hybridities and blurrings that are involved both in their philanthropic roles and in their relationships with government. The final chapter, Chapter Six, draws together some of the main themes and issues addressed in the previous chapters and considers some key questions and difficulties indicated in the earlier chapters. In particular, the chapter focuses on the question whether we can make a case for the shift from government to governance, and argues for an alternative and more precise way of conceptualising this shift through the concept of 'heterarchy'.

Notes

[1] In particular, ESRC research grant RES-000-22-2682.

[2] Dowding (1995) and Marsh and Smith (2000) both suggest that there are four main approaches to the study of policy networks: (1) the rational choice approach; (2) the personal interaction approach; (3) formal network analysis; and (4) the structural approach. The utility of these approaches and of network theory per se is hotly debated and UK policy network literature is peppered with examples of researchers debating, often from different ontological perspectives, the utility of policy network theory to explain policy outcomes. Börzel (1997) also seeks to bring some order to these turbulent methodological waters by suggesting policy networks analyses are described and deployed in three broad, alternative ways:

1. As a metaphor to describe links and interactions between actors involved in the policy process;

2. As a method to analyse social structure, that is, the way in which network structures affect the behaviour of actors and their interactions within that network, so influencing policy outcomes;

3. As an analytical tool to study/analyse the relationships between actors interacting on a given issue.

[3] A significant sub-set of this literature draws upon and relates specifically to the development of multilevel forms of governance within Europe. Given that European policy is developed within networks characterised by a hybrid mix of individual actors embedded in a system of national, subnational, supranational, intergovernmental and transnational relations. The European literature sees 'policy networks as a real change in the structure of the polity' (Besussi, 2006, p 6).

[4] See Ball, 2010c.

[5] These searches are difficult to describe. They begin with individuals and organisations and involve tracing any overlaps or links. For example, a philanthropist may be a trustee of charities, may speak at events or dinners, may be a sponsor or write for the newsletter. These charities are searched – staff, events, publications and so on – other trustees are traced, and their other commitments to 'giving' or business or public service are traced. Events and publications are examined. At each point in the searches other branching links and relationships are followed through until they end. In the interviews the respondents were then questioned about their activities and relationships as identified in the searches.

TWO

Education, network governance and public sector reform

"As part of building the Big Society, we want to open public services up to small and medium-sized enterprises, employee co-operatives, voluntary sector organisations and social enterprises, who may often partner with the private sector. We believe that this will create more innovative and localised services, while also decreasing costs and increasing efficiency. We need all parts of society including businesses, social enterprises and charities to play a part in this radical reform and there's no reason the state shouldn't keep a stake so that taxpayers benefit from the increased value of improved services." (Cabinet Office spokesperson commenting on the *Open Public Services* White Paper [Cabinet Office, 2011a])

In this chapter we will trace some of the developments and changes in forms of governance in England as these relate to the public sector, and specifically education through New Labour (1997–2010) and into Coalition policy (2010–): that is, from the 'Third Way' to the 'Big Society', from government to governance. These changes are multifaceted and multi-scalar and they work at different levels and move at different speeds. They rest upon both structural reconfiguration, the displacement of some actors and organisations and the introduction of others, and the introduction of new working relationships, incentives and subjectivities. They replace bureaucracy with management and leadership, service with 'quality' and 'excellence', professionalism with enterprise and, importantly, 'commitment' with contract. They are moves towards a 'differentiated polity' (Bache, 2003). They restructure the organising principles of social provision right across the public sector. That is to say, the forms of employment, organisational structures, cultures and values, systems of funding, management roles and styles, social relationships and pay and conditions of public welfare organisations are all subject to generic changes. Heuristically these changes may be situated as a part of the transformation that Jessop (1994) represents as from the Keynesian Welfare State to the Schumpeterian Workfare State (SWS).

According to Jessop this transformation replaced the Fordist discourse of productivity and planning with a post-Fordist rhetoric of flexibility and entrepreneurialism. The SWS 'goes beyond the mere retrenchment of social welfare to restructure and subordinate it to market forces' (pp 27–8). For the public sector, this 'involves privatisation, liberalisation, and an imposition of commercial criteria in any residual state sector' (Jessop, 1994, p 30).

All of this is very evident in recent education policy, both in some decisive grand gestures and perhaps more importantly embedded in a variety of mundane and pervasive policy tactics, as in the use of 'best practice', audit, contracts, performance indicators and benchmarks, competition, choice and contestability, and so-called 'workforce reform'. This is not simply about the disarticulation of welfare government: it consists of processes that produce new spaces, states and subjects in complex and multiple forms. Further, the effects of change are not limited to the state itself or to the public sector but also work on and through households, families and communities.

The 'modernisation' of public sector education

Through these changes the landscape of social and education policy has and is being 'transformed' and 'modernised'. This modernisation, which began in the 1970s, accelerated through Thatcherism in the 1980s and the Conservative governments of the 1990s, has been pursued with a single-minded vigour under New Labour since 1997 and is being taken on by the Coalition government. 'From 1947 to around the mid-1970s British welfare was characterised by a system of government: an epoch when, in Kooiman's terms, "Governing was basically regarded as one-way traffic from those governing to those governed"' (May et al, 2005, p 708), with the majority of welfare services provided directly by the state. In the 1970s a process of change began. While the 1979–97 Conservative governments 'broke the mould', the Labour governments of 1997–2010 'reinforce[d]' and 'concretise[d]' the Conservative changes, as Whitty (2006, p 5) puts it, although with a much greater emphasis than previously on the use of performance management as a form of 'strong steering'. Finlayson (2003, p 66) argues that the word 'modernisation' captures the essence of New Labour's social and political project. This modernisation under New Labour was driven by the tenets and methods outlined in *The UK government's approach to public sector reform* (Cabinet Office, 2006). This model is based on four key mechanisms of reform – choice, contestability, workforce reform and performance management (each of these is discussed in some detail in Ball, 2008a) and is drawn directly from the key tenets of New Public Management (see Hood, 1990). That is, New Public Management involves replacing bureaucracy and professionalism with sensibilities and practices drawn from private sector management, like activity-based costing, total quality management, business process re-engineering and notions of leadership, excellence and 'adding value'. The argument put forward by modernisers is that bureaucracy is rule bound, inward looking and risk averse, and is slow to adapt to changing social and economic conditions, while, in contrast, management is innovative, externally oriented, dynamic and enterprising. Professionalism is characterised as paternalistic, mystique ridden, standard oriented and self-regulating, while management is customer centred, transparent and results oriented (see Clarke and Newman, 1997, p 65). New Public Management, then; operates by separating policy from administration – giving managers the 'right to manage' – while at the same time devolving responsibility; uses performance indicators to focus on and measure activity and outcomes; embeds entrepreneurialism in the organisational culture; introduces 'flexible' labour practices; and responds to customer needs and market signals. The UK Coalition government has signalled a variety of ways in which it will push all these aspects of modernisation further and faster in education and across the public services generally.

> We will promote the reform of schools in order to ensure that new providers can enter the state school system in response to parental demand: that all schools have greater freedom over the curriculum; and that all schools are held properly to account. (Cabinet Office, 2010)

This is a modernisation that has already redistributed power and responsibility within the politics of education, away from local authorities both to parts of the central state and to other new and diverse actors and agencies. It is a modernisation based on autonomy and deconcentration, on the one hand, and direction and intervention, on the other – a process that might be termed 'fragmented centralisation' (Monahan, 2005). However, to understand this 'modernisation' fully we need to unpack and examine its facets and components. There is a set of interrelated political *processes* embedded in the dynamics of modernisation – deconcentration, destatalisation, disarticulation, diversification, flexibilisation and centralisation – which have been achieved through a complex series of small *moves* and developments over time (see Tables 2.1 and 2.2). Drawing on Peck's (2004) definition,

Martin and Muschamp (2008) identify 10 elements of the *modernisation* of state education and suggest that 'the process of modernisation is more visible in education than in any of the other welfare services' (p 92).

In education, the Education Reform Act 1988 is ground zero for any consideration of these moves and processes. As Tomlinson (2001, p 46) suggests:

> It made the decisive break with welfare state principles [and] in contrast was about individual entrepreneurism and competitiveness, achieved through bringing education into the marketplace by consumer choice ... It was also paradoxically about increasing the influence of the central state on education by reducing local powers and taking control of what was taught in schools.

More specifically, Powell and Edwards (2005, p 98) list the key features of the Act as follows:

- It gave parents more choice and control over their children's education.
- It increased the power of central government as it relates to education.
- It imposed a centrally directed national curriculum.
- It introduced a national programme of assessment for children at 7, 11, 14 and 16.
- It eroded the power of Local Education Authorities (LEAs), with the introduction of local management of schools [that is, devolved school budgets].
- It constructed a new category of grant-maintained schools financed directly by central government.
- It paved the way for fundamental administrative and financial changes in higher and further education.

Here the relationships between schools, between schools and parents, and between schools and LEAs and central government were all 'unsettled' and the process of disarticulation of the existing system was begun. This is the beginning of what Ainley (2001) describes as a transition 'From a National System Locally Administered to a National System Nationally Administered'; although it could be argued that there is also a process of 'de-nationalisation' involved here. That is, a trend towards a patchwork system, an uneven distribution of types and forms of schooling, both related to local 'needs' and interests and to the serendipity of voluntarism and sponsorship. However, there are two key 'moves' missing from the Education Reform Act agenda, one which had been already announced and one which was added later. First, the introduction of new players into the sponsorship and delivery of state schooling. At the 1986 Conservative Party conference the setting up of 20 City Technology Colleges (CTCs) was announced. CTCs were the invention of Secretary of State Kenneth Baker, who presented them as a 'half-way house' between the state and independent sector. A hundred of the colleges were to be set up across the country, each one funded or 'sponsored' by a business, with spending per pupil far higher than in the schools of the LEAs, from whom they would be entirely independent. Baker told the *Times Educational Supplement* (3 April 1987):

> What we have at present is seven per cent or so in the independent sector, probably going to rise to ten per cent; and on the other side, a huge continent: 93 per cent in the state-maintained sector.... What I think is striking in the British education system is that there is nothing in between ... Now the city technology colleges I've already announced are a sort of halfway house. I would like to see many more halfway houses, a greater choice, a greater variety. I think many parents would as well.

The establishing of CTCs did three things; it contributed to the weakening of the power of the LEAs; extended selection (they were permitted to select some pupils on the basis of 'aptitude'); and involved forms of private enterprise in the running of schools. In the event, only 15 were ever established, mostly backed by individual entrepreneurs; few major businesses were prepared to take part. However, while the CTC experiment might in itself be regarded as a failure, it nonetheless provided a template for New Labour's Academies programme and played a small part in the ongoing destabilisation of the post-war education settlement, creating policy spaces in which education service delivery could be 'thought' differently.

Second, the contracting out of state services to private providers. The significant move here was the setting up of the Office for Standards in Education (Ofsted) as a non-ministerial government department under the Education (Schools) Act 1992 and the contracting out of inspection services to private providers. By the late 1990s over 120 companies held such contracts. These were later reduced to just seven, and in 2009 to just three (awarded to Centre for British Teachers (CfBT), Serco and

Tribal). Again, this, together with other 'moves' (see below), contributed to a change in the possibilities of policy, making the unthinkable possible, and eventually obvious and necessary. This has involved 'an incremental process of breaking up established assumptions and modes of operation and taken for granted practices and replacing these with new "freedoms", new players and new kinds of relationships and new forms of service delivery in many different parts of the education system' (Ball, 2008b, pp 195–6). Bache (2003, p 312) describes this as an 'acceleration' of 'the process of governance' and a 'fragmentation' process which 'undermined the ability of existing powerful institutions, individual LEAs, to frustrate national policy objectives'.

Table 2.1: Processes of public sector transformation

Process	Transformation
Deconcentration	The devolving of budgets and teacher employment to school level.
Disarticulation and diversification	The weakening of LEAs; the introduction of new types of schools (CTCs, Grant Maintained schools, Academies, Trust and Competition schools, new faith schools) and new providers; central funding of CTCs, Academies, Grant Maintained schools.
	Martin and Muschamp (2008) in their analysis of the 'Blair Legacy' of 'modernisation' in education give special emphasis to the abandonment of the comprehensive school as a single template for the state school and the role of diversification. Academies (and other 'sponsored' policies) involve a self-conscious attempt to promote new policy narratives, entrepreneurism and competitiveness in particular. Through these narratives new values and modes of action are installed and legitimated and new forms of moral authority established, and others are diminished or derided.
Flexibilisation	Changes to teachers' pay and conditions of work and employment, and 'workforce reform' – the introduction of 'other adults' into schools and classrooms. The 'opening up' of new routes into teaching, more emphasis on school-based training and the refocusing of teacher education on 'practice' and skills.
Destatalisation	Introduction of new providers by contracting-out of services, programmes and 'policy work', drastically blurring the already fuzzy divide between the public and private sectors, 'reallocating tasks, and rearticulating the relationship between organisations and tasks across this divide' (Jessop, 2002, p 199).
Centralisation	Accumulation of powers to the Secretary of State, abolition of quangos, and central funding of schools.

Together these elements establish a new dispositive: in combination they have 'major repercussions on forms of representation, intervention, internal hierarchies, social bases and state projects across all levels of state organisation' (Jessop, 2002, p 194). We can trace some of the component parts of these processes further through specific policy experiments (Table 2.2).

Within the processes of 'modernisation' and transformation[1] of the public sector, the boundaries and spatial horizons and flows of influence and engagement around education are being stretched and reconfigured in a whole variety of ways. Business is integrated in a number of ways in the governance and provision of state education, in driving innovations and, in effect, disrupting other traditional social relations. This is part of what Pollack (2004, p vii), referring to the National Health Service, calls the 'dismantling process' and asserts to be 'profoundly anti-democratic and opaque'. So, for example, Academies have the opportunity to set aside existing national agreements on the pay, conditions and certification of teachers – the flexibilisation of the workforce. This is a radical move in a more general push for the 'modernisation' of the school workforce – 'workforce re-modelling' – which is now the responsibility of the Training and Development Agency for Schools, one of an increasing number of new 'lead organisations' in the transformation of state education. Through the marginalisation or reworking of local government, professional organisations and trade unions, direct relations are being established between the Department for Children, Schools and Families (DCSF, now Department for Education) and schools and school providers – for example, Academies. Fairclough (2000) argues that the 'dispersal' of government, which was a key feature of New Labour modernisation of the public sector, did not signal an abandonment of close control by the centre, and that this deconcentration rather than devolution is 'not an irrational contradiction, but a predictable consequence of the overall logic' of reform (p 122).

Table 2.2: Modernising moves

Modernising move	Legislation and development	Consequences
Education Action Zones (EAZs)	EAZs were set up following bids from groups of schools. They were partnerships, usually formed between the schools, their LEA and other local organisations, especially from the business community, and other agencies, such as higher education institutions. They were set up to tackle problems of underachievement and social exclusion in disadvantaged areas by devising innovative methods and strategies that would involve disaffected pupils more fully in education and improve their academic performance. Each zone is run by an 'action forum' that involves representatives from the schools and other partners. The forum, set up by statutory instrument, is a corporate body with exempt charitable status. The emphasis was on new activities and combinations of activities that had not been tried together before. The partnership with the business world was seen as a way of bringing the best of successful commercial practice into education, which would create new learning opportunities for teachers and pupils, and raise standards. Twenty-five zones were established by January 1999. A second round of 47 zones started in September 2000. This was followed by an Excellence in Cities (EiC) programme. Twenty-five LEAs and 438 secondary schools were involved in the first phase of EiC. There were two further phases involving 33 LEAs and over 600 secondary schools and some primary schools.	Introduced business influences and relationships into state schooling. Experimented with new forms of local organisation and management of schools.
Specialist schools	The Specialist schools programme is an initiative first introduced by the Conservative government in 1992, but taken up in earnest by New Labour, which encourages secondary schools in England to specialise in certain areas of the curriculum to boost achievement. It was intended that eventually all schools in England would specialise. The SSAT[?] is responsible for the delivery of the programme. Currently there are nearly 3,000 Specialist schools, or 88% of the state-funded secondary schools in England. To become a Specialist school a school had to find £50K of sponsorship, which was then supplemented by government. In 2010 the Coalition government effectively removed this supplement.	Offered a further role to businesses as school partners and introduced a new form of differentiation and branding of schools.

Modernising move	Legislation and development	Consequences
Academies	Academies are state-funded independent schools. They can benefit from greater freedoms to innovate and raise standards. These freedoms include: • freedom from local authority control • ability to set their own pay and conditions for staff • freedom from following the National Curriculum • ability to change the lengths of terms and school days. Prior to the Academies Act 2010, Academies were: • usually in areas of high deprivation, and usually replacing schools which have been deemed unsuccessful • most often, for ages 11–16 and working towards ages 11–18, but all-through schools (3–19) are increasingly common. They were initially supported by an external sponsor, who: • either invested £2 million in an endowment fund (no longer a requirement) or shared its educational expertise • appoints the chair of governors and the principal • selects the academy specialism • develops the educational vision that will inform the academy design brief. Typically, sponsors may be individual entrepreneurs, charities, higher education institutions or further education colleges and may sponsor a single academy or a network of academies (a 'multi-sponsor'). **The Academies Act 2010** The Coalition government decided to allow all schools to apply for academy status. From August 2010, any primary or secondary school judged as outstanding by Ofsted can apply to convert to academy status. From 17 November 2010, schools that are 'good with outstanding features' can apply to convert to academy status. Groups of schools can also apply, provided that at least one school in the group is outstanding or good with outstanding features. Outstanding Special schools have been able to apply to convert to academy status from January 2011. The Academies programme is a good example of the complexity and instability and the experimental nature of these governance reforms. It has gone through at least three iterations, in response to lack of sponsors, rising costs, inefficiencies and opposition. This highlights that within the general logic of reform there is a great deal of muddling through and trial and error.	Introduced a wide range of new sponsors – entrepreneurs, businesses, faith groups and charities. Contracted out these schools to sponsors and removed them from local authority control. Schools funded directly from DfE. Experiments with new forms of teaching and learning.

Modernising move	Legislation and development	Consequences
Competition schools	The Education Act 2006 requires that any local authority wanting to open a new school must put this school out to 'tender', opening up the opportunity for new providers to enter the delivery of state schooling. The first set of these 'competitions' began in Haringey (won by the local authority), and then Southampton (Oasis Trust – a Baptist group), Northamptonshire (Woodnewton – A Learning Community and the Brooke Weston Partnership), Kent (the Homewood Trust – another local school), Lincolnshire (British EduTrust [an Academy sponsor] and the Gainsborough Educational Village Trust), West Sussex (the Bolnore School Group – a parent/ community group), and two in Gloucestershire (one involving the University of Gloucestershire and supported by the White City Project and a cluster of local churches in the Gloucester City Deanery).	Introduced new, local providers and partnerships – a precursor to 'Free Schools'. Allowed Academy 'chains' to expand and diversify.
School companies	Sections 11 and 12 of the Education Act 2002 enable governing bodies of maintained schools to establish companies for specified purposes. Ninestiles School has set up a school company under the 2002 legislation, called Ninestiles Plus. The school is the lead school in a federation that also includes Waverley School and the International School, all in Birmingham. Ninestiles Plus was established to respond to the many requests received from secondary schools around the country to visit Ninestiles School and/or to take part in its training courses on school improvement.	Introduced enterprise into school organisation, bringing new sensibilities into play, and new sources of income.
Federations	The Education Act 2002 introduced a number of measures designed to help schools to be more innovative. One aim was to bring schools together in a collaborative arrangement to raise standards, promote inclusion and find new forms of teaching and learning. Any type of education provider can agree to work with another, formally or informally, including further education institutions, independent schools, Academies and CTCs. However, only maintained schools can federate under a single governing body.	Allowed for new relationships among schools and other educational institutions, both as an alternative to the local authority structure and as a model for kinds of provision (for example, for-profit school chains).

Modernising move	Legislation and development	Consequences
Contracting out LA services	The Conservatives gave Ofsted powers to inspect LEAs in 1996 and New Labour used these inspections to identify 'failing' LEAs. Procedures in the Schools Standards and Framework Act 1998 enabled the Secretary of State to bring private education companies into the management of failing LEAs. The first such contract was awarded on 1 July 1999 to the Stock Exchange listed education company Nord Anglia to run the School Improvement Service in Hackney, which was in its turn found by Inspectors to be inadequate. These contracts normally arose from serious concerns about LEAs' performance and capacity, identified in Ofsted (see Campbell, Evans et al, 2004) and subsequent 'recommendations' made by consultants (PriceWaterhouseCoopers in many cases) to the DfES. Consultants are also employed to write the resulting contract when private contractors were used. However, not all authorities in difficulties have been out-sourced and out-sourcing was one of a number of 'experiments' by the DfES to encourage 'new ways of working' by LEAs. The evaluation of these 'experiments' by Bannock Consulting (Bannock, 2003) identified 11 interventions leading to outsourcing; 11 interventions of other kinds; 10 New Models funded by the DfES; and 11 independent innovations. Several of these experiments involved private companies as partners (for example Surrey/VTES; CAPITA worked with Oxfordshire, West Berkshire and Wokingham). Swindon and Haringey, which were contracted out, have subsequently returned to local authority control. Hackney is outsourced to a not-for-profit trust and Education Leeds is run on a not-for-profit basis by CAPITA. Bache (2003, p. 308) describes these outsourcings as 'experiments with ways of improving service delivery'.	Furthering weakening of local authorities and further roles for the private sector in the management of public services, and experiments with new forms of organisation of local services.
Contracting out policy programmes/ services	Policy programmes is a rather loose category used here to refer to national schemes of various kinds that are contracted out to private providers. These can range from information technology and management systems to pedagogical or curriculum initiatives. Among the former are various system management contracts held by CAPITA, including PLASC (Pupil Level Annual School Census), TPS (Teachers' Pension Scheme – £62m), ILAs (Individual Learning Accounts – now terminated), school admissions, education smartcards (£100m over seven years) and Children's Trust accounts (£430m over 20 years). CAPITA is the specialist provider of such services. In 2005 CAPITA also took over the contract for the National Learning Strategies (Literacy and Numeracy) from CfBT (worth £177.5m over 5 years).	Replaced direct services with contracted services in heartland of policy, with concomitant reductions in central staffing of education. Contracts have also given government more flexibility in funding and system steering, through the use of non-renewal or cancellation of contracts.

Modernising move	Legislation and development	Consequences
Trust Schools	The Education and Inspections Act 2006 included the provision for a Foundation School to set up a charitable foundation (or trust) to support the school. This type of Foundation School is known as a Trust School. To acquire trust status, existing foundation schools can set up a charitable trust. Community Schools can take on foundation status and set up a trust within a single process. Schools can set up a trust in a collaborative group whereby the schools acquire foundation status and adopt the same trust. The aim of Trust Schools is to use the experience, energy and expertise from other schools and professions as a lever to raise standards in schools. Trust Schools remain local authority-maintained schools. As of January 2009 the total number of planned Trust Schools was 444, with 124 already open.	Again introducing new players into school governance, with different perspectives and methods – for example, the Co-Operative Society is involved in 104 schools trusts.
Benchmarks and targets	National testing and the publication of school examination performance in the form of league tables have provided an infrastructure for top-down performance management. New Labour appointed a Schools Standards minister in 1998 and began to set benchmarks and targets for national achievement levels. Benchmarks for schools have also been set, based on 5+ A–C grades at GCSE, originally 15% in 2000, raised to 30% in 2008 and 35% in 2010; the indicator itself has also been changed. Those falling below the benchmark are deemed to be 'failing schools' and subject to closure, intervention or redesignation (as Academies).	The setting of national targets is also indicative of the reconceptualisation of the education system as a single entity and as a fundamental component of national economic competitiveness (Ozga, 2008).
Free Schools	Free Schools are a Coalition government initiative very loosely modelled on Sweden's independent free schools. According to the DfE website: 'Free Schools are all-ability state-funded schools set up in response to what local people say they want and need in order to improve education for children in their community.' According to the Anti-Academies Alliance, by mid-August 2010, applications for 62 Free Schools and 153 schools wanting Academy status had been received by the DfE. The work of liaising and supporting groups interested in setting up Free Schools has been 'out sourced' to the New Schools Network (NSN, see Chapter Five). In October 2010 the DfE announced £500,000 funding for the work on the NSN. In March 2011 the Chancellor, George Osborne, set aside £50 million for Free Schools' capital funding.	Introduces a very different group of new players and provides opportunities for existing players to expand their participation. Also part of the Coalition's localism agenda, enabling parents, community groups and local charities to open and run their own schools.

Note:
a SSAT – The Schools Network:
We work with schools throughout England, and in 36 countries across the world, to raise achievement for all students (3–19 years).
We are an independent, not for profit charity. All our resources are invested and reinvested in supporting the school system.
Over 90% of English mainstream secondary schools, almost 50% of special schools, and 600 primary schools are members of SSAT.
We are the largest membership organisation for academies and converter academies and have been championing innovation in the schools system for over twenty years.
Our aim:
We aim to give practical support to transforming education by building and enabling a world-class network of innovative, high-performing schools in partnership with business and the wider community. (www.ssatrust.org.uk/whatwedo/Pages/default.aspx, accessed 21 February 2011)

Tony Blair indicated the role and nature of these changes and the general logic of New Labour's public sector reforms in his speech in 2005 introducing the Labour government's White Paper on secondary education:

> In our schools ... the system will be finally opened up to real parent power. All schools will be able to have academy style freedoms. All schools will be able to take on external partners. No one will be able to veto parents starting new schools or new providers coming in, simply on the basis that there are local surplus places. The role of the LEA will change fundamentally ... Where business, the voluntary sector, philanthropy, which in every other field is a part of our national life, wants to play a key role in education and schools want them to, they can. (Blair, 2005)

Perhaps we can also think about these processes and the logic of reform by borrowing and adapting Tickell and Peck's (2002) heuristic formulation of the development and spread of neoliberalism, that is, what they call *roll-back* and *roll-out* neoliberalism. The first, *roll-back*, involves a destabilising and restructuring of existing state services and a progressive withdrawal of the state from the active delivery of welfare and towards a more 'mixed economy' of educational provision. The second, *roll-out*, is a shift towards a more socially interventionist agenda and the creation of a policy infrastructure that is conducive to the participation of new providers and that privileges the rationales of enterprise in general and business more specifically. Here, though, the role of the state itself is crucial as market maker, animator and performance manager – involving a giving up of 'direct' control in favour of 'effective' control (Davies, 2002, p 315).

Central to this modernisation, as indicated already, is a process of substitution and the creation of modes of entry for new providers – a process that replaces traditional public sector actors with others (businesses, charities, voluntary organisations and social enterprises) and that at the same time replaces traditional public sector values and sensibilities (service) with others (enterprise and entrepreneurship). As Tony Blair put it in his 1998 address to local government: 'If you are unwilling or unable to work to the modern agenda, the government will have to look to other partners to take on your role.'[2] The remainder of this chapter and, indeed, the remainder of this book focus on the implications and consequences of Blair's comment and the role of 'other partners' in state education services and in education policy.

Specifically we are concerned with the role of philanthropy as a new kind of 'partner', but, as will become apparent, philanthropy is not distinct from either social enterprise or business as a field of action in relation to the state. Previously Ball (2007) focused specifically on the role of business in education network governance and service delivery.

Philanthropy, business and modernisation

In the last 25 years philanthropic activity has played an increasing and significant, but still minor, role within the processes of public sector modernisation. It is one contributing factor to the processes and discourses of changing educational governance, one site (or set of sites) among others that has served to validate, circulate and reiterate new discourses and practices, and one component in a new infrastructure of public service delivery. Nonetheless, we want to suggest that philanthropy has played a particularly important symbolic and strategic role. Symbolically, philanthropy provides an 'acceptable' alternative to the state in terms of its moral legitimacy. Under both New Labour and the Coalition charitable giving, social investment, social enterprise and volunteering have been given particular emphasis (see Chapter Three). It has also provided a kind of rehabilitation for forms of capital that were subject to 'ill repute' in the public imagination. Strategically, philanthropy has provided a 'Trojan horse' for modernising moves that opened the 'policy door' to new actors and new ideas and sensibilities. As discussed further in Chapter Three, 'new philanthropy' carries with it the perspectives and methods of business, and of finance capital in particular. It is self-reforming, becoming much more business-like itself, and also has a transformative effect upon the services with which it becomes involved. Some of the initiatives and moves that have involved charities have established forms of relationships and models of provision that lend themselves to further stages of privatisation or for-profit participation (for example, Academy chains).

Let us ground and relate together some of these elements of philanthropic engagement by looking at a local example of 'network governance'. This example, which begins in Northamptonshire, also illustrates the layering, complexity and multifaceted nature of the new roles, relationships and responsibilities embedded in these new arrangements for service delivery and policy (see Figure 2.1). This network diagram focuses on the Garfield Weston Foundation (GWF), the charitable trust of British Associated Foods – which is recognisable in the UK through brands like Primark, Twinings and Kingsmill.

Figure 2.1: Garfield Weston Foundation

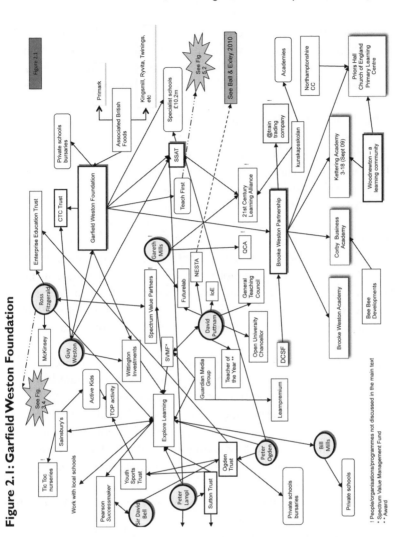

In a relatively simple sense this network illustrates some of the complexities and blurrings involved in the shift from government to governance. The GWF is 'engaged' here with public sector education in a number of ways through different sorts of relationships, and in different kinds of partnerships, both local and national. GWF is a school sponsor: it has donated £10.2m to sponsor specialist schools and to support the SSAT (Specialist Schools and Academies Trust); it also supports Teach First (see Chapter Five). The SSAT is a 'link and lead' organisation and a para-statal organisation that has assumed many aspects of the work that had been previously done, in different ways, by LEAs (see note 1). Guy Weston, who is chairman of Wittington Investments (see below), is a former chair of the SSAT.

GWF also runs a bursary scheme that funds state school students to attend private schools. Overall, in 2009 it made cash donations totalling £37.6m in areas ranging from the arts to the environment. GWF also works with the de Capell Brooke family trust as Academy school sponsors, The Brooke Weston Partnership (BWP) and is running three Academies in Northamptonshire. As the BWP website explains:

> The Brooke Weston Partnership is a response to today's climate where leadership and management of secondary schools are becoming more complex and challenging. Recognising the benefits to be gained by collaboration the partnership brings together a number of schools each with its own principal but operating under the leadership of an 'executive principal'. (www.brookewestonpartnership.org/)

The first of these schools, the Brooke Weston Academy, was initially a CTC and is a partner in sponsoring the other two. In addition, one of these other two, the Corby Academy, is run in partnership with Bee Bee Developments, a property and construction company that owns the land on which it is built.

> Bee Bee Developments has been granted planning permission for Priors Hall, the ex-quarry site in Corby, including 5,100 homes, 63,000m² of commercial space, three primary schools, a Government Academy designed by Foster and Partners and 500 acres of parkland. (www. beebeedevelopments.co.uk/area.php?title=Corby)

In the third Academy, the 3–18 Kettering Academy, the BWP works with a local state school, Woodnewton – a Learning Community – to deliver the primary stage. In 2008, together with Woodnewton, the BWP bid for and won a competition to run Priors Hall Church of England Primary Learning Centre. Another local school, Oakley Vale Primary, is a BWP associate school. GWF is, then, involved in four different initiatives and moves that engage philanthropic partners in forms of experimentation in and modernisation of public sector education – CTCs, Specialist schools, Academies and Competition schools. These involve partnerships with business (Bee Bee) and local authority schools (Woodnewton).

There are two other 'old style' Academies in Northamptonshire: one the Northampton Academy, sponsored by the United Learning Trust, a Church of England charity; the other The Malcolm Arnold Academy, sponsored by the David Ross Foundation (Ross Frozen Foods). In August 2010 the Coalition government announced £55m of funding for two new build Academies (Kettering Science and Kettering Buccleuch), and as of 23 May 2011, 16 Northamptonshire schools have applied to change their status to become 'new style' Academies (see Table 2.2 and below).

Looking at another section of the network, the investments that support the GWF are handled by an investment vehicle called Wittington Investments. In 2000 Wittington invested in a new commercial venture called Explore Learning. Other investors included the Guardian Media Group and, acting in a personal capacity, Sir Peter Ogden, Sir Peter Lampl and Bill Mills. Sir Peter Ogden launched the Ogden Trust with a £25m donation, to improve educational opportunities for lower-income families – principally by providing bursaries to attend private schools. The Trust also supported a CTC and has sponsored 57 Specialist schools with grants totalling £985,000 (as of January 2008) and it sponsors an Academy (Healing School). Sir Peter Ogden is a trustee of the Specialist Schools and Academies Trust (SSAT). Sir Peter Lampl is founder of the Sutton Trust, which has the aim of providing better educational opportunities for lower-income families. Its principal activity is funding summer schools at leading universities, targeted at teenagers attending secondary schools with a poor history of sending students to top universities. More generally, the Sutton Trust researches and explores 'solutions' to social mobility in education. Sir Peter also supported the access of low-income students to Belvedere GDST School, and encouraged its transfer to Academy status. He also sits on the SSAT board. (Both Sir Peters might be good examples of what du Gay (2008) calls 'anti-elitist elites'). Bill Mills is founder of Brookham School – a private pre-prep school for 3- to 7-year-olds. He is also chairman and owner of Highfield School, a prep school in Hampshire. The Guardian Media Group has an education subsidiary, learn.co.uk, which runs Learnpremium, a teaching and learning resource website for schools covering a wide range of subjects from Foundation to AS level. The Guardian Media Group holds its investment through the Spectrum Venture Management Fund, on whose board sits David Puttnam (a Labour peer), the founding chairman of the General Teaching Council 2000–02 (abolished by the Coalition government in 2011) and appointed as chancellor of the Open University in 2006. He was chairman of NESTA (the National Endowment for Science, Technology and the Arts) (see below) from 1998 until 2003 and is also chairman of Futurelab. Explore Learning is a growing network of 49 store-front tutorial centres based in Sainsbury's stores.[3] Explore Learning uses Pearson *Successmaker* software, and Sir David Bell, a director of Pearson, is a trustee of the Ogden Trust. Both the Sutton and Ogden trusts are benefactors of the Youth Sports Trust, which has a partnership with Sainsbury's through its TOP programme, which is an extension of the Active Kids Campaign. The Ogden Trust has also made donations to the Enterprise Education Trust (Deutsche Bank and PriceWaterhouseCoopers also donate), which ran the Ogden Trust National Schools Business Competition; and Ross Fitzgerald, founding chairman of Explore Learning, is a trustee of the Enterprise Education Trust.

Here, then, is a set of complex relationships replete with overlap, multiplicity, mixed ascendancy and blurred boundaries between public, private and philanthropic actors of different sorts, with those involved moving between and operating with different roles in different spheres. These relationships involve a diverse set of processes (exchanges), partnerships and interdependencies rather than constituting a structure. It is an example of dispersed and re-spatialised policy action, focused on new sites of influence, decision making and delivery. Business interests, philanthropy and the public service are tightly intertwined and there are complicated issues of purpose, ownership and control embedded here. The actors are linked socially and commercially and through their philanthropy and public service in and through their different capacities. Locally and nationally they are implicated in the disarticulation of state education and, we would argue, in new forms of governance in the roles that they play in 'steering, setting directions and influencing behaviour' (Parker, 2007, p 114). In other words, these are 'not just networks' (Parker, 2007), and are more than just a loose arrangement of actors involved in talk (Marinetto, 2003). Although not all of the elements of the network have a governance function, the movements and interactions involved serve to consolidate social relations and provide opportunities for social interaction. This is one small part of, a glimpse of, a more general shift from the 'hierarchy of command' to a form of 'polycentric' and 'strategic' governance that is based upon network relations within and across new policy communities designed to generate new governing capacity and enhance legitimacy. We can also discern here a more basic process of the commodification of education, for example, through the work of Explore Learning and the role of education provision in Bee Bee's housing development and sales strategy, which shifts perceptions and appreciations of the nature of education and makes it more amenable to for-profit exploitation. The form of such networks and relationships and governance capability varies from locality to locality – this is just one example. While in education the establishment of 'new governance' is uneven and experimental, it is also, for the time being at least, inexorable. It is introducing new players and agents, a set of new languages and practices, new interests and opportunities/commitments and new 'authorities' into public sector education (see Table 2.2), while also changing the meaning of what public sector education is. It relies on new forms of sociality and institutional configurations and new values. At its core, the techniques of network governance, 'Privatisation, franchising, outsourcing and deregulation may all be conceived as governmental drives to distribute authority to numerous state and non-state units that assume the economic enterprise form' (Shamir, 2008, p 6). All of this involves an increased reliance on subsidiarity and 'regulated self-regulation', and it drastically blurs the already fuzzy divide between the public and the private sectors.

Education and the labour market

We are suggesting here that arising from the interrelationships between network governance, public sector reform and new responses to social problems there is a general disarticulation of state systems. One of the key facets of this, which is one of a number of infrastructural possibilities intended to facilitate the entry of new providers, introduce new ways of working and new organisational forms, and perhaps achieve cost reduction, is the weakening or breaking up of national agreements on pay and conditions of work, and the concomitant weakening of trade union influence and national pay bargaining arrangements. In education this has been a general trend over a number of years, with the introduction of endogenous flexibilities to allow schools to pay teachers differently and weak but multifaceted forms of performance-related pay. Again, this weakening is a process made up of numerous small moves and inroads. For example, the *Five Year Strategy for Children and Learners* (DfES, 2004) emphasised the link between so-called new professionalism (see below) and pay by asserting that 'career progression and financial rewards will go to those who are making the biggest contributions to improving pupil attainment, those who are continually developing their own expertise, and those who help to develop expertise in other teachers' (DfES, 2004, p 69). As a result, recommendations from the Rewards and Incentive Group – a sub-group of the social partnership that advises on pay and performance management provisions – led to each school in England and Wales undertaking a complex and time-consuming pay restructuring. Alongside this, the National Workload Agreement (DfES, 2003) began a process of workforce reform that allows cheaper and sometimes minimally qualified Learning Support Assistants into classroom work and other student-related activities. While the National Union of Teachers (NUT) never signed the agreement and the National Association of Head Teachers (NAHT) withdrew from the agreement in 2005 and rejoined early in 2007, the other four unions, the Association of School and College Leaders, the Association of Teachers and Lecturers (ATL), the National Association of Schoolmasters/Union of Women Teachers, and the Professional Association of Teachers have consistently remained as signatories.

These 'moves' have been ramified by further exogenous flexibilities introduced through the Academies programme, and latterly the Free Schools programme. Hence:

> ATL is concerned about working time provisions which have appeared in new contracts in some of the academies. We have heard reports of academies introducing a working year of 1,400 hours, extending the length of the school day and reducing the lunch break to 30 minutes. There is also concern over top-heavy management structures in some academies.
>
> ATL's concerns were reflected in a report by PriceWaterhouseCoopers, commissioned by the government and published in June 2005. The report states: 'Staff workload is generally heavier in academies compared to the previous schools'. The report also referred to tensions arising from having staff employed on different contracts within the same academy.[4]

These new schools [Free Schools] will be academies, which are publicly funded independent schools, free from local authority control. They will enjoy the same freedoms as traditional academies which include setting their own pay and conditions for staff, freedom from following the National Curriculum and the ability to change the lengths of their terms and school days.[5]

Some Academy providers recognise unions for pay negotiations, others do not; some providers have honoured transition agreements, others have not; some have honoured these arrangements only for existing staff. The other general and longer-term significance of this deconcentration and flexibilisation relates to the interests of for-profit providers. In schools, salaries are the major component of running costs, around 80% of budget. It is here that cost cutting related to potential profitability will be sought by reducing pay, introducing longer working hours or substituting lower-qualified and lower-paid staff for better-qualified, higher-paid staff. Alongside this, the use of forms of performance-related pay 'focuses' teachers' work ever more firmly on classroom 'productivity', and specifically on the generation of 'outputs' for institutional performance indicators. This is part of the general process of subsidiarity involved in network governance that is linked to new forms of 'steering' and central performance management, but that at the same time offers new 'freedoms' to providers, changes the labour process of teaching and further disarticulates the systemic underpinnings of state education.

> Current educational reforms in England and Wales mark a new phase in the restructuring of state education. The labor process of teaching, that in the past has been shaped and re-shaped by reform policies focused on school organization and curriculum re-structuring, has now itself become the direct focus of change. These reforms are cast in terms of a 'new professionalism' in which teachers focus on the core task of teaching and learning in which financial rewards are closely related to teachers' ability to demonstrate their impact on pupil progress, and in which teachers have access to high quality professional development. All this is located within the context of a new and constructive relationship between 'social partners' in which the foundations of new professionalism are determined by dialogue and debate rather than conflict and strife. (Stevenson et al, 2007, p 7)

Towards the Big Society?

As many commentators have already noted, the trajectory of Coalition policies in many areas of social policy involves an extension and elaboration of New Labour initiatives rather than a rupture or distinct change of direction (see Bochel, 2011), in the same way that New Labour took on and pursued many of the trends and principles of Conservative policies when it came into government in 1997. For the sake of the argument of this book we will concentrate on these areas of continuity (see Exley and Ball, 2011 for further discussion of differences). Nonetheless, there is a change of emphasis, at least in rhetoric, with even greater attention being given by the Coalition to diversity, to 'freedoms', to less bureaucracy and to localism, although these were all evident under New Labour. The Coalition Secretary of State for Education explained:

> ... all schools, whether or not they are making the journey towards academy status, are being given greater freedoms from central government. We have abolished the self-evaluation form, reduced the data collection burden and told Ofsted to slim down its inspection criteria. We will be slimming down the National Curriculum, making governance simpler and financial management less onerous. All of these steps will give school leaders more freedom to concentrate on their core responsibilities – teaching and learning. Different schools will go down different paths, at different paces. (Michael Gove to the National Conference of Directors of Children's and Adult Services, 4 November 2010)[6]

New Labour certainly sought to develop 'new approaches to empowering citizens ... fostering new professionalism [and] providing strategic leadership' (Cabinet Office, 2008, p 11). In education, it paid particular attention to parental choice, and flirted with ideas like 'Personalisation' (Charles Leadbeater, Demos), 'Self-directed public services' (Charles Leadbeater, Demos), 'new localism' (Stoker, 2000) and 'the collaborative state' (Demos, with Innovation Unit and NCSL) (see Ball and Exley, 2010). All of this is being taken forward by the Coalition and a new language of reform is being deployed. The Secretary of State for Education explained in a speech in 2010, that the Coalition government's reform programme:

is driven by two principles shared across the coalition parties. We believe in shifting power down from central government to the lowest possible level – to local authorities, schools, mutuals and co-ops, GP consortia, community groups, families and individuals.

...

Progress depends on encouraging creativity, making services more responsive to individual citizens, allowing valid comparisons between different providers to be made and using transparency – not central direction – to drive value for money. (Michael Gove to the National Conference of Directors of Children's and Adult Services, 4 November 2010)

To realise these principles new legislation is being put in place, but also various aspects of the Labour infrastructure of public sector reform are to be put to further use (see also Chapter Three for a discussion of other aspects of continuity and development between the Third Way and the Big Society). David Cameron reiterated his pledge to 'end the state monopoly in provision of public services' in a *Daily Mail* article, previewing a White Paper that would establish a 'presumption that private companies, voluntary groups or charities are as able to run schools, hospitals and many other council services as the state' (*Daily Mail*, 21 February 2011). This seems like a direct reiteration of Tony Blair's warnings and pledges quoted above. Indeed, further, in echoing the New Labour commitments to meritocracy and central regulation, Cameron added that the state would still have a role in ensuring 'fair funding, ensuring fair competition, and ensuring that everyone – regardless of wealth – gets fair access' (*Telegraph*, 20 February 2011). The Coalition also has a 'social mobility strategy', and on 5 April 2011 in the House of Commons, Deputy Prime Minister Nick Clegg told MPs that improving the life chances of children born into low- and middle-income families is the government's 'overriding mission'.

In education, symbolically at least, it is the Coalition's Free Schools initiative (see above) that has garnered most attention. Again though, it can be argued that this is nothing more than a further 'move' of deconcentration and disarticulation that builds upon Labour's Academies and Trust and Competition schools. The first 16 Free Schools were announced 7 September 2010 and included five proposed by faith groups, two involving ARK, and one each by The Childcare Company, King's Science Academy and Discovery New School. Five more were announced in November 2010. According to the Anti-Academies

Alliance, by mid–August 2010 applications for 62 Free Schools and from 153 schools wanting Academy status had been received by the Department for Education (DfE). By September 2011, 30 Free Schools had been approved to pre-opening stage or had signed funding agreements with the DfE, and the first 24 schools opened. As noted already, the work of liaising and supporting groups interested in setting up Free Schools has been 'out-sourced' to the New Schools Network (see Chapter Five) – the title itself is significant, as is the tactic. We can 'see' something of the work of network governance embedded in and under-pinning this initiative in the DfE 'Free Schools Conference' held on 29 January 2011. Michael Gove addressed the conference about 'Visualising a new school landscape'. Rachel Wolf, director of the New Schools Network, spoke about 'Submitting a proposal – best practice', and Joel Klein, CEO of the Educational Division of News International, and representatives of the US Knowledge is Power Programme (see Chapter Five) and the Washington DC Public Charter School Board, talked about 'Learning from the best: international evidence'. Four hundred and four people are listed as attending the conference. Some of these were from what we will come to recognise in this book as the 'usual suspects': 17 from Teach First (Chapter Five), 8 from Future Leaders (Chapter Five), several Academy providers and people from Policy Exchange (a Conservative think-tank) (Chapter Five), 14 from Waldorf, Steiner and Montessori schools, as well as solicitors (there is money to be made from the transaction costs arising from setting up new schools), CfBT, Cognita (a private school chain), Kunskapsskolan, National Association of Independent schools, National Governors Association, SSAT, several private vocational training companies and theatre and film schools, 18 from the DfE, an enormous variety of trusts and charities (for example Filmer Trust, Flowers Trust, Future Educational Trust, BBG Community Trust), and groups involved in making proposals for Free Schools (for example Neighbourhood School Campaign, We need a School, Scream Theatre School, Fingerprints Primary School Planning Committee). However, the largest single set of organisations represented would appear to be faith groups: a minimum of 58 (some designations are not clear), of all types of faith. Who was missing is also interesting and significant: no unions and no public sector organisations were represented, and there was just one person from a university.

Here we can glimpse networking and network development in a new 'site' of policy, one that is typical perhaps of the methods of network governance – a closed event, opaque, almost unnoticed. Events like this are occasions for establishing intricate interdependencies and shared dialects, for building trust and drawing boundaries. Rhodes (1996) and many others argue that trust is a key coordinating mechanism in network governance, but the potential for conflict also needs to be acknowledged (Davies, 2005) and the form and content of relationships involved in this example are enormously diverse and multifaceted and not easy to classify. There is a mix of lasting ties and episodic collaborations that link local projects to national policy goals through varied and complex forms of interaction. This is a moment of network evolution, the construction of new 'collaborative spaces' (Skelcher, 2007). Importantly, it is possible again, as with the GWF example, to identify overlaps, recurrences and multiple relationships that relate to other 'bits' of policy and reform. For example, one of those attending was Mark Goodchild from the New Schools Fund, an initiative of the Salisbury Partnership, a social enterprise of which Nat Wei is a partner (he is Big Society adviser to David Cameron and co-founder of Teach First, see Chapter Five). Sites like this construct, join up and maintain an epistemic policy community, reaffirming existing ties and making new exogenous connections. The international 'lessons' that were deployed serve to 'stabilise' a particular set of 'rationalities, metadiscourses and logics' that have been 'instituted as the basis for action' (Larner, 2003, p 760). There is a mix of openness and 'normative compliance' (Skelcher, 2007). There were also various 'boundary spanners' (see Chapter Four), brokers and 'thought leaders' or 'policy entrepreneurs' in attendance – like Rachel Wolf, David Triggs (Academies Enterprise Trust), Mike Feinberg (Knowledge is Power Program, KIPP) and Tim Byles (Partnerships for Schools). Events like this and the networks in which they are embedded are, as Clarke and Newman (2009, pp 92–4) put it, 'complex assemblages, combining and condensing different forms of power'. These experiments in network governance bring new players into the policy process at all levels and further diminish the role of public sector organisations, qualified practitioners and elected local government, although the latter is also being given new roles, but reduced funding, by the Coalition. Maile and Hoggett (2001, p 512) argue: 'Local government is increasingly becoming a "policy free zone" ... [its role] to deliver centrally determined policies in a strategic way.' In a different lexicon this is a microcosm of the Big Society (which is discussed more fully in the following chapter), populated by charities, voluntary and community groups seeking to participate in and control local services. Here there are 'new kinds of educational alliance' (Jones, 2003 p 160), an extension of those which 'New Labour [sought] to create' around 'its project of transformation' and which mobilise various resources in the borderland between the public, private and voluntary sectors and move towards a more interactive, fragmented and multi-dimensional form of policy making. These events and networks are a policy device, a way of trying things out, getting things done, changing things, and a means of interjecting practical innovations and new sensibilities into areas of education policy that are regarded as change resistant and risk averse. In general terms they 'pilot' further moves towards a public service system in which increasingly the state contracts, devolves and monitors rather than directly delivers education services, using 'performance' measurement, benchmarking and targeting to manage a diversity and patchwork of provisions.

Governance and governing

The new forms of governance outlined above are most obvious in the sponsorship and founding of new sorts of schools within the state sector – Academies, Free Schools and Trusts – but are not confined to these programmes and initiatives. Nonetheless, these new schools do point up quite dramatically the shift in the role of the state from 'directing bureaucracies' to 'managing networks'. The Academies programme and Free Schools initiative are now being used by the Coalition government to bring about a general break-up of the state system and of the relationship between schools and local authorities. They are part of a more general process of gradual but steady deconcentration and destabilisation, a process of creating greater autonomy (for example, autonomous schools directly related to central government) and at the same time reinforcing direction and intervention by allocating more power to the centre – 'hollowing out' and 'filling in' at the same time. Indeed, 'far from the centre being hollowed out, resulting in a permanent loss of capacity, there is a growing emphasis in the core executive [and] on strategic co-ordination' (Taylor, 2000, p 46). Indeed, Skelcher (2007, p 44) argues that the move away from a 'state-centric view' is 'overstated' in the governance literature. This is something we will return to in the final chapter.

The Academies Bill, passed in July 2010, has enabled the expansion of Academies beyond secondary schools into primary and special schools ranked 'outstanding' by Ofsted, removing the need for local authorities to be consulted. Later announcements have indicated the determination of the Coalition government to further extend the programme by providing academy routes for almost every category of school: 'Alongside outstanding schools, all schools that are ranked good with outstanding features by Ofsted will automatically be eligible for academy status. All other schools – primary or secondary – that wish to enjoy academy freedoms will also be eligible, providing they work in partnership with a high-performing school that will help drive improvement.'[7] In this context, 142 schools will be converting to Academies in the school year 2010–11, including 7 primary schools, and 74 new Academies that will replace 'failing' schools. Michael Gove announced that he would impose Academy status on failing schools 'where I judge that academy status is in the best interests of an eligible school and its pupils, and where it has not been possible to reach agreement on a way ahead with the local authority, the school or both'.[8] This represents a significant expansion carried out at unprecedented speed. 'One new academy is being created every working day' (David Cameron, Prime Minister's Questions, 24 November 2010),[9] which the DfE highlights as 'record progress; it took five years for 15 city technology colleges to open, and four years for the first 27 academies to open'.[10] As of January 2012 there are now 1,529 open Academies in England.

The move from government to governance involves a set of changes in the form and modalities of the state, and a set of new relationships within and to the state – vertical and horizontal – involving new actors and new interests and purposes and the insertion of new rationales and practices into state welfare provision (Ling, 2000) in a framework of 'constrained discretion' (Stoker, 2004, p 166). Also being embedded and realised here are new forms of regulation and power. The different elements of change are interrelated and interactive, they facilitate and open up the possibility of new moves, new opportunities, new subjectivities, ethics, logics and commitments. However, this is not a ruptural move from one spatio-temporal fix to another but, as noted, an on-going roll-back/roll-out process, which is unstable but which is creating a new field of political rationality. As Jessop (2002, p 199) says: 'there is nothing new about parallel power networks that crosscut and unify the state apparatus and connect it to other social forces. But this reliance has been reordered and increased. The relative weight of governance has been increased at all levels …'. In the remainder of this book we explore how this new 'fix', this new governance, works, who is involved, how they relate, what they do, and to some extent why they do these things, focusing on education as a 'case', but set within a more general landscape of social and political change.

Notes

[1] See also Loughlin, 2004.

[2] www.solarnavigator.net/prime_minister_tony_blair.htm.

[3] www.explorelearning.co.uk/vebo/.

[4] www.atl.org.uk/pay /pay-background/pay-background-academies.asp.

[5] www.education.gov.uk/schools/leadership/typesofschools/freeschools/ freeschoolsfaqs/a0075639/free-schools-faqs-types-of-free-school.

[6] Available at www.education.gov.uk/inthenews/speeches/a0066543/ michael-gove-to-the-national-conference-of-directors-of-childrens-and-adult-services.

[7] www.education.gov.uk/inthenews/inthenews/a0068023/gove-announces-expansion-of-academies-programme.

[8] Speech to the National Conference of Directors of Children's and Adult Services, available from https://sites.google.com/a/antiacademies.org.uk/aaa/ Home/headlines/govetoforcestrugglingschoolstobecomeacademies.

[9] *Guardian*, 24 November 2010, Politics Live with Andrew Sparrow. Available from www.guardian.co.uk/politics/blog/2010/nov/24/pmqs-davidcameron.

[10] www.education.gov.uk/inthenews/pressnotices/a0064203/142-schools-to-convert-to-academy-status-weeks-after-academies-act-passed.

THREE

'New' philanthropy, social enterprise and public policy

"It's part of their tradition [Goldman Sachs] and, secondly, they make a huge, an outrageous amount of money for working there. So the combination of the two means that a lot of those guys are very active philanthropically. They've got the money and there is sort of a feeling that, I think, if you work at Goldman, that you don't just put all that money in your jeans, you're supposed to be doing something useful with it. That's the combination." (Sir Peter Lampl)

Introduction

In this chapter we will explore some of the contemporary entanglements of 'new' philanthropy with social and education policy and, concomitantly, some of the ways in which:

> commercial enterprises increasingly perform tasks that were once considered to reside within the civic domain of moral entrepreneurship and the political domain of the caring welfare state, dispensing social goods other than profits to constituencies other than their shareholders. (Shamir, 2008, p 2)

The chapter is a *pot pourri* organised around the theme of enterprise and the discourse of enterprise: enterprise in philanthropy, philanthropy and the enterprise curriculum, and philanthropy and social enterprise. The latter pursues the relationships between philanthropy, the Third Way and the Big Society indicated in the previous chapter. We also hope to illustrate more of the connections between philanthropy, education policy and governance, and the social and interactive density of the philanthropic community itself. We argue that the discourse of enterprise in its various forms is a crucial component, both as a reforming narrative and as an effective infrastructure, of network governance.

As indicated in the previous chapter, the boundaries between philanthropy, business and the public sector are being moved and blurred, the public sector generally is being worked on and reworked by new policy actors, from the inside out (endogenous change) and the outside in (exogenous change). This is happening in particular through the dissemination of the values and practices of enterprise and entrepreneurship and the transposition of the 'international discourse of managerialism' (Thrift, 2005, p 33) and its metaphors, that is New Public Management, into the public sector and through attempts to *embody* those metaphors in the public sector workforce. New values and modes of action are thus being installed and legitimated and new forms of moral authority established, while others are diminished or derided. This is also a process of substitution both of actors and of values. As indicated in the previous chapter, philanthropy in its various forms is currently a key device in the reconstitution of the state and of governance, or of what Jessop (2002, p 240) refers to as 'the organisation of the conditions for governance'. This is, as he goes on to argue, 'a process of muddling through' (p 242), or what might be considered as the 'orderly disorder' of network governance, which involves:

> Defining new boundary-spanning roles and functions, creating linkage devices, sponsoring new organisations, identifying appropriate lead organisations to coordinate other partners, designing institutions and generating visions to facilitate self-organisation in different fields.

However, the arrangements, relationships, means and forms of exchange within new forms of governance are becoming increasingly and quickly more orderly and sophisticated. We have already offered some examples of the new roles, partners and lead organisations and forms of self-organisation that embed, legitimate and facilitate new governance in education. In this chapter we will begin to get a little more 'inside' governance, through a focus on the roles and functions of some 'new' philanthropies and by exploring some of the 'reforming' discourses that philanthropy brings to the remaking of relationships, practices and methods of organisation within or in place of the public sector. While education policy analysis has paid some attention to some recent 'philanthropic' interventions – most obviously the role of philanthropies and philanthropists as sponsors of Academy Schools (see Gunter, 2010) – there has been neither much consideration of such interventions as examples of the work of 'new' philanthropy per se nor therefore much examination of the discourses through which such interventions are articulated and which they bring to bear (Woods et al, 2007). The point is that these discourses 're-form' the objects about which they speak. As we shall suggest, 'enterprise' is one key discourse here that joins up endogenous and exogenous change in the public sector and does the work of 'reflexive redesign of organizations' (Jessop, 2002, p 242) and contributes to the 're-modelling' of teachers and students as enterprising subjects, and legitimates and facilitates 'new' solutions to 'wicked' social problems.

In particular we will look at the engagement of corporate financial organisations, like Goldman Sachs (see Figure 3.1) and HSBC (Figure 3.2) in philanthropic activity and consider, in passing, some of the motives and purposes underpinning such activity. In the first case the focus is on individuals as philanthropic actors, in the second case the focus is in a corporate foundation. This will lead to consideration in the next chapter of the participation in and influence on policy of 'boundary-spanning' philanthropic actors. The emphasis in this chapter is on breadth rather than depth; we hope to 'map' the spread, mutation and polyvalency of 'reforming' discourses across and within public policy and the public sector in a very general way.

We will also sketch in some features of the infrastructure of possibilities and incentives set of place by New Labour and built upon by the Coalition to facilitate philanthropic and social enterprise participation in public service funding and delivery. However, we begin by defining what is new in 'new' philanthropy.

'New' philanthropy

Philanthropy itself is being reformed. What is 'new' in 'new philanthropy' is the direct relation of 'giving' to 'outcomes' and the direct involvement of givers in philanthropic action and policy communities. That is, a move to a more 'hands on' approach to the use of donations; "they [donors] want to be involved in the way the project is managed, for example" (Amanda Spielman, ARK). Thus, one of our interviewees distinguished between palliative and developmental giving. The latter being about "something that needed doing in the world and giving money was doing something about it … if you've got a certain number of pounds or dollars then these people want to put them where they will have most effect" (Spielman). These new sensibilities of giving are based upon the increasing use of commercial and enterprise models of practice as a new generic form of philanthropic organisation, practice and language – venture philanthropy, philanthropic portfolios, due diligence, entrepreneurial solutions and so on.

As Handy (2006, p 1) puts it, 'Generosity is fashionable again.'[1] *The Times* now publishes a 'giving list' as well as a 'rich list' and the 30 most philanthropic individuals on the list in 2006 gave almost £0.5bn between them; by 2008 this had risen to £2.38bn; but in 2011 this total fell back to £1.67bn, although the number of givers donating more than £10m and £1m had increased. Handy suggests that 'Philanthropy has almost become the new status symbol. To have your own foundation or a wing of a building named after you can be an outward and respectable mark of success' (Handy, 2006, p 9). There has also been a recent flurry of foundings of new corporate philanthropic organisations and individually funded trusts and foundations (see below for some examples). Most of the major UK corporate charities have been founded since 1995, and many since 2000. In many cases the development of philanthropic activity by major corporates and multinationals is part of a larger 'investment' in corporate social responsibility (CSR) and community programmes. These are now taken very seriously by most major corporations. A secondary infrastructure has grown up to support CSR as an 'industry' in its own right (see www.csrwire.com/) and there is a related academic literature (Crane et al, 2009). CSR activities, it is argued (for example, see 'What's Wrong with Corporate Social Responsibility?', www.corporatewatch.org.uk/?lid=2670), serve the interests of companies in a variety of ways, ranging from reputation management to risk management and employee satisfaction (this was highlighted in a number of the research interviews). Ben and Jerry's was the first company to publish a 'social report', in 1989. These are now standard (for example, http://annualreport.kpmg.eu/corporate-social-responsibility.htm).

> "It starts off with the value statement, what binds all the KPMG member firms together is the values. So we have a set of seven values, which is how we operate. One of those is that we are committed to our communities, and how we interpret that depends on different geographies." (Mike Kelly, KPMG)

> "We do recognise the business benefits as far as principally, frankly, what it means to our people and our staff engagement with the organisation. It's very important to them that we have those kind of moral values, so that we're undertaking that. But we've always steered very well clear of in any way crossing the boundary for these activities to

be – for us to be accused of these being a marketing activity, a PR activity." (Peter Bull, HSBC)

Through both CSR programmes and individual philanthropic action, companies 'assume socio-moral duties that were heretofore assigned to civil society organizations, governmental entities and state agencies' (Shamir, 2008, p 4). Alongside the CSR activities of corporations there has also been a proliferation of corporate-funded (for example Private Equity Foundation (PEF), Absolute Return for Kids (ARK), Support and Help in Education (SHINE)) and individual foundations and trusts (for example, Ogden, Beecroft, Harris) that are focused on educational issues.

A further aspect of 'new' philanthropy is what Sir Peter Lampl, founder of the Sutton Trust, calls 'strategic philanthropy'. According to Sir Peter, there is a real opportunity for philanthropists to get the government interested in innovative projects. "Where a project has proven its efficacy, we work closely with government to try to secure nationwide uptake and funding. I have invested money in demonstration stage projects, and, in partnership with the media, have tried to persuade the government to take these demonstrations and scale them up at a regional or national level." He went on to say: "I'm looking to try and persuade the government to do things that we think make sense ... we evaluate them carefully and then we're trying to get wider implementation" (see Ball, 2011 for a further example of strategic philanthropy). The argument is also made that philanthropists and charities can be "more flexible than governments about modifying and developing what they do ... start small and expand gradually and change what they're doing in response to early-stage feedback – a different sort of developmental model" (Spielman). SHINE (see below) is a good example of this 'smart', hands-on approach to giving. All of its projects are looked at in terms of the possibilities of 'replication'; for example, Nrich (Millennium Maths project): 'Shine grants have funded delivery costs for the trial and demonstration phases of this project and a comprehensive evaluation that will be used to look at if and how the project could be rolled out' (SHINE website, www.shinetrust.org. uk/site/pages/8_projects.php); and the Family Literacy Development programme that 'has been piloted in two schools and SHINE is funding all the costs associated with rolling it out to additional schools in the London Boroughs of Southwark, Lambeth and Wandsworth' (SHINE website, www.shinetrust.org.uk/site/pages/80_previousgrants.php).

One Academy sponsor who was interviewed explained that his company wanted to "create an environment in which we can continue testing ideas and continue evolving and from which we can influence practice in other places". The second aspect of this 'new' philanthropy is the use of forms of business research and due diligence to identify or vet potential recipients of donations, and the use of metrics and other indicators to monitor the impacts and effects of donations on social problems. As Stephen Shields, then chief executive of SHINE, explained, they "interview schools or organisations to see if we think they're fit to run one of our projects that we know already works" and "we track and evaluate everything", or as Sophie Livingstone, then of the Private Equity Foundation, put it, "we agree milestones and KPIs [key performance indicators] for the lifetime of the investment", which involves "applying the techniques and tools of private equity". The philanthropists themselves want to see clear and measurable impacts and outcomes from their 'investments' of time and money. In relation to its 2011 'giving list' the *Sunday Times* and Charities Aid Foundation asked donors a number of questions; in their responses 89% of donors said they were interested only in charities that could clearly demonstrate the impact of their work, and 72% reported spending a considerable amount of time researching their philanthropic choices (*Sunday Times*, 20 May 2011). In this way the business perspective is brought to bear upon educational issues and problems. This is indicative of a generic shift within business philanthropy towards forms of strategic and development philanthropy based on the methods of private equity investment, another mix of caring and calculation:

> "So they are business oriented and not just gently philanthropic and we'll give money to people. They want results and they want measured results but they will wait for those results. And I'm trying to persuade PEF, for example, that although they've put a lot of their money into – quite rightly – into stuff that will help NEET [not in education, employment or training] young people, now I also want them to be thinking about how they help the nought- to eight-year-olds who will be the NEETs of the future as a parallel strategy." (Jean Gross)

A service infrastructure has developed to undertake research and evaluation of charities to provide information for donors and for charities themselves, again based on private sector practice, and a market in private, for-profit advice for donors is emerging. The highest-profile organisation in this field is New Philanthropy Capital (NPC), a social enterprise 'consultancy and think tank dedicated to helping funders and charities to achieve a greater impact' (website) that was set up by a group of partners from Goldman Sachs (see Figure 3.1).

> "But because I had been involved with that [NSPCC] I got involved with New Philanthropy. Their origins, I think you would say, and you would have heard this from others, were the, sort of, the rational economists in the ranks of Goldman Sachs who wanted to know why people didn't put more store by making smart investment decisions in philanthropy." (Jon Aisbitt, Goldman Sachs and the Man Group)

John Copps, Head of Sector Research at NPC, explained:

> "the idea is that one of the reasons the private sector works reasonably efficiently is that there's information and analysis so investors can seek the highest return, whereas if you turn to charities and you want to make a social return there's no information ... there's a lack of connect between how good a charity is, its results, and then its ability to generate money, its ability to get income from donations ... we exist to produce information and analysis. And so two aims, really, to guide donors and to also help charities themselves get better at measuring and demonstrating their impact and using that to improve their work. We do the investment analysis-type stuff, but obviously you are not buying shares you are donating ... it's like any professional service."[2]

New philanthropy also involves the deployment of business strategies and methods, particularly those of venture capitalism, in relation to social problems by the funding of innovative and sometimes 'risky' solutions to 'wicked' social problems. Funders will normally expect to see a 'return' on their 'donation' but accept that some risky 'investments' will fail. Peter Lampl sees the Sutton Trust as "run a bit like a private equity firm ... we look at opportunities that come through the door, we initiate opportunities and we make a decision about where we're going to put our resources". This is sometimes called 'philanthrocapitalism' (*Economist*, February 2006), that is, the idea that charity needs to start to resemble a capitalist economy in which benefactors become consumers of social investment. 'This is an integrating business approach to spurt an entrepreneurial spirit for the welfare of humankind' (http://observer. bard.edu/articles/opinions/216). Business donors see themselves having a "philanthropy portfolio" (Amanda Spielman). A further development of this kind of approach is the introduction of the possibility of a financial return on 'investments' in solutions to social problems, as in the case of the Social Impact Bond (see below) – "what it's going to do [as one example] is use private funding to finance interventions with kids coming out of prison" (Peter Wheeler, Standard Chartered, Social Impact International).

Handy goes further in recent writing, to describe what he calls 'new new philanthropy', that is:

> Hedge fund and private equity managers who via their own foundations, choose to 'invest' their donations in other charities and projects and use the latest money-market strategies, research tools and techniques to manage the performance of their portfolios. (http://www. managementtoday.co.uk/news/741088/the-new-new-philanthropists/)

Goldman Sachs

Figure 3.1 offers some (simplified) sense of the philanthropic activity of corporate finance, in this case focused on Goldman Sachs (individual and corporate), and also, in this case, educational philanthropy in particular. Education is only one dimension of the philanthropic interests of such corporations and their senior executives. We also begin to see here (as a snapshot) something of the sociality of philanthropic networks, the joined-upness and embeddedness (Granovetter, 1985) of the participants (see Chapter Four), but as a social morphology rather than as a social structure, based on common histories and shared narratives. Social, business, philanthropic and political relationships are intertwined and interlayered here, and function in relation to one another: "it's a bit of chicken and egg, you don't know whether the CSR engagement grows from the business engagement or the business engagement grows from the CSR engagement" (Mike Kelly, KPMG). Trust is important here, as a 'joint performance by those who are deemed to be "in the conversation"' (Urry, 2004), business relationships are carried over into philanthropic ones and they are mutually reinforcing. There is also plenty of 'co-present interaction' (Shamir, 2008), indeed corporate philanthropy is driven by social events, like dinners and awards, opportunities for 'talk and touch', which beget trust (see Chapter Four).

"And some friends within the private equity industry, one of them phoned me up and said – he's a trustee of one of the NSPCC [National Society for the Prevention of Cruelty to Children] fundraising committees – said, 'The NSPCC have asked me if I'll organise a private equity dinner for the NSPCC and just wondered what you thought about that.' And I said, 'I've been to this ARK dinner, seen it, and I really think that we should have a private equity dinner or a charity of which the NSPCC could be one of the beneficiaries, or should be because this is why you're involved, but it should be a private equity dinner, not an NSPCC dinner, for the private equity industry. It's a private equity industry dinner for charity.' And about eight of us in total got together and said, 'You know, we really should do this, we should do something about this'." (Charlie Green, Candover Equity and PEF)

There is a mixture of strong and weak ties in these networks of philanthropy, which need to be 'kept up'. All of this gives a 'thickness' and a particular social texture to these networks. The relationships within them work on several planes and interface at different points within business itself and in the social and the political. It is possible to glimpse in the networks some of the opportunities for 'influence' in relation to policy – through positions, memberships and relations (with government, parties and politicians) (see Chapter Four). These engagements offer a wide variety of 'commitments/opportunities' (Urry, 2003, p 164) to speak to government and speak about policy (FutureBuilders, London Development Agency, City Leaders Group, see Chapter Four). There are also a number of network nodes evident in Figure 3.1, both organisations (Goldman Sachs, NPC, ARK, and SHINE) and people, that are 'boundary-spanners' – whom Williams describes as 'key agents managing within inter-organizational theatres' (2002, p 104). There are also actors here who move and make their careers across sectors. The relationships embedded here and the spheres of activity and influence stretch across local, regional, national and, indeed, international settings (for example Social Impact International, Atlantic Philanthropies, Goldman Sachs Global Leaders programme). Several of the actors are engaged 'across' the range of philanthropic activity, from donation (sponsors), to representation (board members, trustees), infrastructure (NPC, The Big Give, Social Finance) and service delivery and programmes (SHINE, Greenhouse, Academies, Social Impact). These sites and their relationships are where new discourses are

Figure 3.1: Goldman Sachs

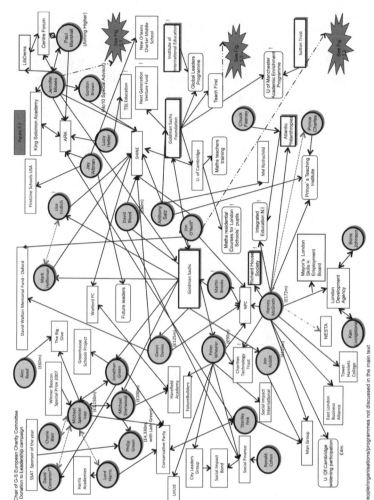

* Chair of G–S European Charity Committee
** Donation to Leadership campaign

! People/organisations/programmes not discussed in the main text

articulated and shared and through which they flow. Links and relations here can also be traced to all three main political parties (Jennifer Moses: Labour and Lib Dems; Michael Spencer and Jonathan Green: Conservatives; Peter Wheeler and Jon Aisbitt: Labour). The New Labour Academies programme appears – the Harris Academies, Harefield Academy, and Jon Aisbitt's abortive attempt to sponsor an Academy in Brighton, as does in various forms their *widening participation* in higher education initiatives. There are also connections with and donations to various universities. The network is thus associated and implicated in various ways with educational reform and processes of modernisation.

The second example (Figure 3.2) is a more specific case – SHINE. SHINE is a charity founded by a group of Goldman Sachs partners (Jim O'Neill, Mark Heffernan and David Blood) using some of the monies they received when Goldman was floated on the Stock Exchange in 1999. The 200-plus partners continue to receive significant annual bonuses, which in the mid-2000s were an estimated $10m each. SHINE focuses its attention on education, as co-founder Jim O'Neill explains, for a mix of personal and business reasons:

> "As an economist I believe unless you can raise the productivity of people in your society you can't boost long-term growth and welfare. And of all the ingredients that matter the most important thing is education. And secondly because of all my own personal upbringing, I knew that the thing that distinguished me from many people that I grew up with was my education."

SHINE is a donor and supporter of other initiatives like Teach First, Every Child a Reader, Enterprise Education Trust and so on and a receiver of donations – from Lehmann Brothers, 100 Women in Hedge Funds, KPMG Foundation, the Sofronie Foundation, Generation Investment Management LLC and so on, and is a funder of new programmes (see below). It works with voluntary and public sector organisations, and has links to the 'great and the good' (Prince of Wales, Sarah Brown, Sir Alex Ferguson, David Beckham, Alistair Campbell). Sir Peter Ogden (see below) and Dame Alison Richards (vice chancellor, University of Cambridge) are also patrons, Anthony Salz is a trustee. SHINE provides a good example of the social texture, boundary-spanning and joined-upness of philanthropic networks. Through funding, people and events it is linked to an interrelated set of social and political initiatives that involve social enterprise and venture philanthropy. It is assuming socio-moral duties, addressing problems of social and educational disadvantage and contributing to a reworking of the landscape of educational provision, that is, funding organisations that seek to take on the work of the public sector, and it is funding programmes that, if successful, can be scaled up by government.

> "We thought we would be prepared to fund risky things that the government didn't really have an obligation to consider on a mass basis. And our whole ethos was, and sort of remains, to finance projects that we think we can measure and really show that they influence kids for the better, with the eventual goal being getting government to take it over." (Jim O'Neill)

In different ways all of the primary discourses of 'new' philanthropy are represented in the work of SHINE. We move on to look at these next.

Philanthropic discourses

Three key and interrelated discourses appeared repeatedly in the research interviews and in the educational programmes and activities of corporate philanthropies. One articulates a concern with issues of *social disadvantage*, another is *meritocracy* and the third is *enterprise* or *entrepreneurship*, but the three discourses can be seen to have a relationship and constitute a loose but coherent 'discursive ensemble' that articulates a particular vision and purpose for education. In the simplest sense, educational philanthropy can provide opportunities to students and families with talent or ability whose education is inhibited by disadvantage. Foundations like Garfield Weston and The Ogden Trust offer bursaries to students or to schools to enable 'able' but under-privileged students to attend private schools. In the latter case there is a special emphasis on science and maths. In a number of cases this kind of commitment reflects the personal experience of individual philanthropists and gives rise to a hybrid of individualism and communitarianism that is focused on the issue and problem of social mobility – which is the primary concern of the Sutton Trust (see, for example, its Universities Summer School programme www.suttontrust.com/projects/university/sutton-trust-summer-schools/).

Figure 3.2: SHINE

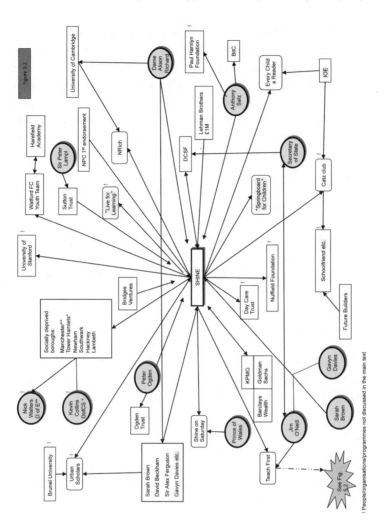

"I came from a working-class background and I still think that social mobility through education has definitely declined through the last ten or fifteen years. Is it the grammar schools? I don't really want to make an argument to reinstate grammar schools. But the issue is, true social mobility through education has declined and that's something we should be very worried about." (Peter Ogden)

"...you know, your social origin should not end up being your life destination. It just goes against everything that I think is fair. And therefore my educational focus has always been on how I can help other people to have the same advantages that I had. Had I not got a free place at Manchester Grammar School ... [It's] that belief in equality of opportunity and that belief that some people just never, ever get a chance to find out what they're good at and how good they can be." (Jon Aisbitt)

The philanthropies seek to address the problems of young people, particularly those of 'high ability', whom they see as not currently well served by the state system.

"We focused in on what the trust [HSBC Global Education Trust] should – what its main criteria should be. And we saw that as being disadvantaged young people, financial literacy, international understanding and the teaching of languages." (Lorraine Thomas, HSBC Global Education Trust)

SHINE has three points of focus for its work.

"Those are the three areas that we fund in: 'behind', 'in the middle' and 'gifted' and capable of flying, but really being held back by socio-economic circumstances. We brought on some gifted projects so that we could look more at the aspirational side of things, so for children who maybe don't have the support at home, maybe don't have the IT infrastructure at home. A lot of children on the projects that we fund that involve gifted have been given no experience of anybody else who's ever been to university. I read a high percentage of some of the young people – on the Nrich programme, I think it was – didn't know a single other young person who had been to university." (Stephen Shields, SHINE)

Alongside these concerns with social disadvantage and meritocratic opportunity, for some philanthropies entrepreneurship is seen to be and is offered as a potential route from disadvantage to opportunity – in some cases, again, this is a reflection of the personal experience of 'self-made' philanthropists but is also presented as an attempt to remedy the failure of state education to teach and instil the values of enterprise. For corporate philanthropies this is also in part a reflection of their particular business interests.

> "Schools are doing much more creative things and giving them opportunities, but then it's not taking them forward to the next level ... you know for us, as a major recruiter, attitude is the all-important thing." (Lorraine Thomas)

The philanthropic engagements here involve the insertion, in various modes and guises, of the sensibilities of enterprise into education – an enterprise curriculum, in effect. Indeed, enterprise education now has internationally all of the infrastructure and trappings of a school subject – teacher training programmes, advanced courses, professional associations, journals, manuals and texts; the Institute of Education has a Department of Geography, Enterprise, Mathematics and Science. Taken together, this constitutes a recontextualising context, in Bernstein's terms (see Brant and Falk, 2007). The enterprise curriculum, in the broadest sense, is an attempt to rework students through the 'formation of an entrepreneurial identity' (Axhausen, 2002) and, indirectly at least, draw them into the ambit of financial capital as workers or customers. Enterprise Education is now a ubiquitous global phenomenon that is typically linked, in particular in government policy texts, to international competitiveness in the knowledge economy. (Holmgren and From (2005, p 387) see entrepreneurship education 'as one realisation of the neo-liberal oriented restructuring process, which is sweeping through Europe'.) Again, examples of corporate philanthropic involvement will have to serve as illustration here (see Figures 3.2 and 3.3).

One example of such activity, which operates on a global scale, with member organisations in 40 countries, is SIFE (Students in Free Enterprise): its strapline is 'A Head for Business. A Heart for the World'. SIFE's mission is 'a diverse network of university students, academic professionals and industry leaders around the shared mission of creating a better, more sustainable world through the positive power of business'

Figure 3.3: HSBC Global Education Trust

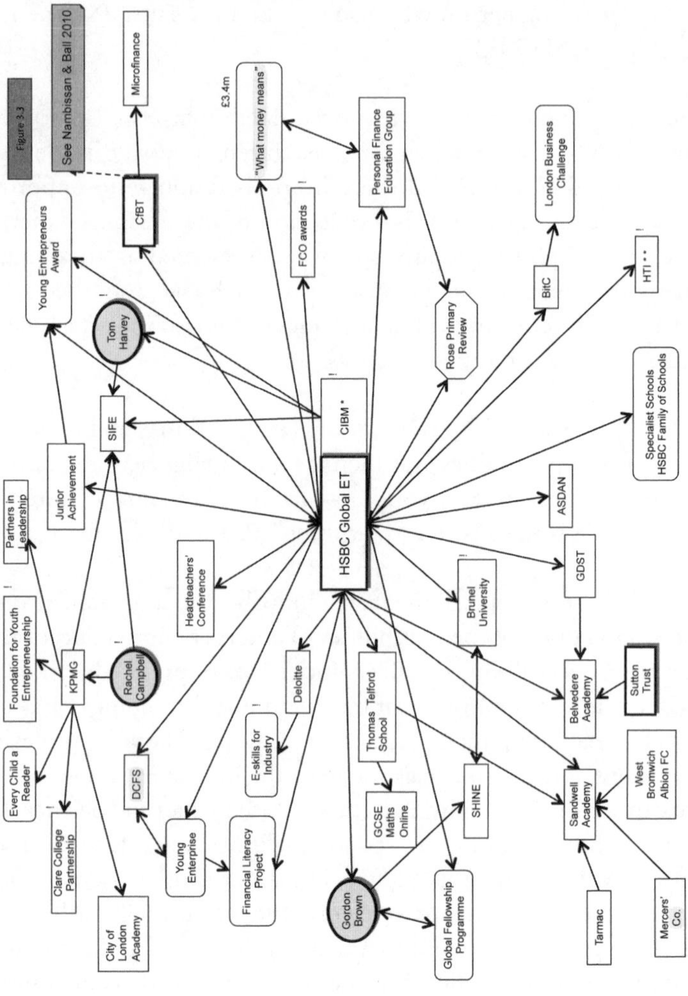

See Nambissan & Ball 2010

Microfinance

£3.4m

"What money means"

Personal Finance Education Group

London Business Challenge

Young Entrepreneurs Award

CfBT

FCO awards

BitC

HTI [* *]

Tom Harvey

SIFE

CIBM [*]

Rose Primary Review

Specialist Schools
HSBC Family of Schools

Junior Achievement

Partners in Leadership

HSBC Global ET

ASDAN

Foundation for Youth Entrepreneurship

Headteachers' Conference

GDST

KPMG

Rachel Campbell

Brunel University

Every Child a Reader

DCFS

Deloitte

Thomas Telford School

Belvedere Academy

Sutton Trust

Clare College Partnership

E-skills for Industry

Young Enterprise

GCSE Maths Online

SHINE

Sandwell Academy

West Bromwich Albion FC

City of London Academy

Financial Literacy Project

Gordon Brown

Global Fellowship Programme

Tarmac

Mercers' Co.

* Corporate, Investment Banking and Markets division
* * Heads, Teachers & Industry

| People/organisations/programmes not discussed in the main text

(www.sife.org/AboutSIFE/Pages/AboutSIFE.aspx). SIFE's 'world headquarters' is in the US, but both HSBC and KPMG are major sponsors. As an example: PUC Campinas (Pontifical Catholic University of Campinas) in Brazil has developed a programme with SIFE students called *Expert Kids$*, taught to underprivileged and economically deprived 7- to 10-year-olds in Campinas, which is based on the HSBC Financial Literacy Programme. The Campinas programme teaches about 'the financial facts of life, the basics of money and how to save and invest and use it wisely' (PUC website). Also, in a partnership with Laurier University in Canada, PUC and SIFE 'Students brainstormed and found a local Brazilian product that could be marketed and sold in Canada, emphasizing the importance and complexity of international business' (SIFE website).

Junior Achievement (JA) is a similar organisation with a longer history. It was founded in the US in 1919 by two company presidents. Today JA 'claims to reach 8.3 million students per year ... in more than 100 countries' (Holmgren and From, 2005, p 387) with a curriculum that ranges from pre-school to college level and covers work readiness, life skills, financial literacy and entrepreneurship and mini-business programmes, using TV and interactive websites.

Kids Speak Out About Entrepreneurship

More than half of kids 13–18 want to start their own business someday. And, to prepare for that, nine out ten of them believe that entrepreneurship should be taught in school. (www.ja.org/)

Sukareih and Tannock (2009, p 782) argue that the principal goal of JA is 'to instil a deep and lasting commitment to free market principles in the minds, habits, dreams and ambitions of young people everywhere'.

HSBC has an extensive portfolio of educational philanthropy through its Global Education Trust and its CSR division, HSBC Communities. Alongside the involvements noted above, HSBC has worked with the Personal Finance Education Group to develop a curriculum programme for schools called 'What Money Means'.

"It's about starting to inform children at an early age about some of the issues about money. Not talking about the complexities of budgeting or ISAs or anything like that, but talking about some of the issues like needs and wants and those kind of choices that you have to make and things like that. Now, as part of that we're working in partnership with a charity called the Personal Finance Education Group, PFEG, who are indeed working directly with the government, with the Department for Children, Schools and Families, on other elements of their work. So we are telling the government what we're doing, we're going in front of them and talking to them about what we're doing and why we think it's important [...] we are engaging with, for instance, the Rose review, which has just reported on the primary school curriculum." (Peter Bull, HSBC)

HSBC has also sponsored over a hundred specialist schools, at a cost of over £3m, was an inaugural supporter of the Specialist Schools and Academies Trust and has been a corporate supporter of Teach First since 2003.

HSBC, a long-term supporter of the independent education charity Teach First, today welcomes students from three secondary schools to their Canary Wharf offices. The pupils are the winners of a business skills and maths challenge, created specially for Teach First by the SIFE (Students in Free Enterprise) society at the London School of Economics, and supported by HSBC.[3]

The Trust is also a partner sponsor of two Academies: Belvedere, in which Sir Peter Lampl is involved; and Sandwell, with partners Tarmac, West Bromwich Albion FC, Thomas Telford CTC and the Mercers' Company. The Sandwell Academy has a Sport and Business Enterprise specialism. HSBC also sponsors the Young Entrepreneurs Awards and the Young Enterprise Innovation Awards. With SIFE, HSBC has also funded and run a Global Financial Literacy Programme in 29 countries: 'Improvements in financial literacy can not only support social inclusion, but can also enhance the contribution the financial services sector makes to the world's economy.'[4] HSBC has also worked with the charity Young Enterprise for 25 years: 'Each year, our business volunteers inspire over 250,000 young people aged 4 to 25 years. Our programmes empower the next generation with the confidence, ability and ambition to succeed in a rapidly changing global economy' (website). It also collaborates with the education social enterprise ASDAN to develop personal finance courses. It runs an annual conference for the head teachers of its family of schools.

"We invite about 100/120 head teachers from both state schools and independent schools, because we also support scholars around the world, but particularly in the UK. And so it's an opportunity for them to network as well …"
(Lorraine Thomas)

One point of focus and advocacy and development for the enterprise curriculum in the UK is the Enterprise Education Trust (EET) (see Figure 3.4), which runs among other activities the Network for Teaching Entrepreneurship, which has among its sponsors UBS, Warburg, Apax Holdings, Garfield Weston and Deutsche Bank. It also runs the Harris Academy Business Challenge in collaboration with PricewaterhouseCoopers volunteers.

The Harris Academy Business Challenge was created with our long term corporate supporter PricewaterhouseCoopers LLP (PwC). Over 100 volunteers from PwC shared their knowledge of business and financial planning, project management and presentation skills during their London volunteering week at the beginning of June. (EET website, www.enterprise-education.org.uk/home.php?mod=show_news&id_nws=33)

The Ogden Trust funded for a time the National Schools Business Competition, which was run by the EET. In Scotland the Hunter Foundation funds the University of Strathclyde Centre for Entrepreneurship and co-funds with the Scottish Government the Schools Enterprise Programme. Also in Scotland, Charles Skene funds the Skene Enterprise Trust, which organises the Skene Young Entrepreneur Award and funds the Robert Gordon University Centre for Entrepreneurship. Teach First runs a "social entrepreneurship programme, to help ambassadors start good social enterprises that will make a real impact in the classroom in addressing educational disadvantage" (Brett Wigdortz).

Returning to the EET, this organisation is related on a number of levels to discourses of enterprise: social enterprise banking (Social Finance, Bridges Ventures, UnLtd); the teaching of enterprise in schools – Network for Teaching Entrepreneurship, Global Entrepreneurship Week, Achievers International; and social enterprise education and campaigning more generally. One of EET activities, Business Dynamics, was founded in 1977 by 3i, the venture capital company. Business Dynamics is chaired by Sir Paul Judge and 'aims to bring business to

Figure 3.4: Enterprise Education Trust

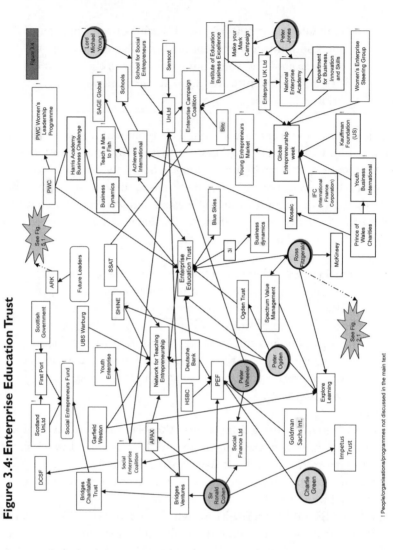

! People/organisations/programmes not discussed in the main text

life for young people. Volunteers from companies introduce students, aged 11–19 years, to the opportunities and challenges of business as well as improving their skills in preparation for the world of work.'[5] EET serves as a focus of, and is indicative of, the interconnectivity of sites of enterprise advocacy and development, and their relationships to business. There is a separate, more public sector-focused enterprise education network focused around the National Education Business Partnership Network, Enterprise Village and DfE-funded Enterprise Network (www.enterprisevillage.org.uk/partners/iebe/).

These sites, programmes and events are conduits for the enterprise discourse. They point up both the role of businesses in developing and supporting curriculum development and curriculum interventions, as well as the complex global flow of ideas and funding through networks established by philanthropic and educational organisations. They also give some indication of the increasingly subtle and complex relations between moral and business interests in the forming of particular kinds of financially 'responsible' and entrepreneurially competent citizens and workers through education. Gibson (2008) argues that this is part of a broader socio-economic project that 'fetishises market forces' (p 68) and requires the adaptation of human actors to them. Within these educational discourses, Gibson suggests: 'Human actors or people are things to which events occur' (p 69) or are rendered into a set of psychological traits that make up 'enterprising people' (p 71). Here, as Shamir (2008, p 8) puts it, business assumes moral authority and agency and mobilises 'designated actors actively to undertake and perform self-governing tasks' and perfect their own human capital (Sukarieh and Tannock, 2009, p 782). Referring to 'enterprise' in the specialisms of Academy schools, Woods and colleagues (2007, p 254) make the point that what is happening through these various 'incursions' into the school curriculum is a form of 'enclosure' wherein 'areas in the public domain are being carved out for enhanced private influence over the symbolic and cultural power to shape educational purposes and practices'. They go on to argue that, as a result, the boundaries between public control and private influence are being tested and are becoming increasingly unstable.

Alongside its inroads into the school curriculum, business philanthropy is also importing other forms of enterprising sensibility into school organisation through the dissemination of leadership and business practices (see, for example, the Partners in Leadership programme in Chapter Four). In the same way, as described earlier, that philanthropy is being reworked by the sensibilities of business and business methods, these sensibilities and methods – New Public

Management – are also being installed in diverse ways into the organisation and curricula of educational organisations. Indeed, the enterprise model for organisational practice and its concomitant values and perspectives, or what Gordon calls 'the ethos and structure of the enterprise form' (Gordon, 1991, p 44), are being proselytised and are disseminated through the networks and relationships outlined above as a generic form for all types of social organisation and social relation. Through philanthropy, business partnerships and government initiatives, 'it is enacted in a multitude of programmes, strategies, tactics, devices, calculations, negotiations, intrigues, persuasions and seductions aimed at the conduct of the conduct of individuals, groups, populations – and indeed oneself' (Rose, 1999, p 5). Enterprise is positioned as neutral and necessary for reform, for effectiveness and for problem solution. Enterprise works not just to tie education to economic imperatives in a variety of ways, but also it articulates and produces a distinct conception of the human actor. It is 'the model of the active citizen [as] one who [is] an entrepreneur of him- or herself' (Rose, 1999, p 164). Social enterprise is one aspect of what Shamir (2008, p 6) calls the 'economization of the social', within which government becomes a facilitator of a 'market of authorities'. 'Government itself becomes a sort of enterprise whose task it is to universalize competition and invent market-shaped systems of action for individuals, groups and institutions' (Lemke, 2001, p 197).

Banking on social enterprise

Social enterprise is of course the space in which philanthropy and business meet, or meet again, a squaring of the circle of public sector reform.

> Social entrepreneurs combine the savvy, opportunism, optimism and resourcefulness of business entrepreneurs, but they devote themselves to pursuing social change or 'social profit,' rather than financial profit. (http://davidbornstein. wordpress.com/faq/)

Social enterprise is 'a novel image for a mode of activity to be encouraged in locales which had previously operated according to very different logics' (Rose, 2007, p 20). Social enterprise indeed has been a particular realisation of New Labour's Third Way and has been a key discursive trope within the intellectual community that informed New Labour thinking (see Ball and Exley, 2010). As Walker (2007, p 56) puts it: 'Reconciling socialism and capitalism, the third way was about harnessing entrepreneurial drive within a context of social and public purpose. The third sector has become the third way in action.' In 2007 the Department for Trade and Industry (DTI) reported that there were 55,000 social enterprises in the UK with a combined turnover of £27bn, making up 5% of all businesses and accounting for 1% of GDP (Walker, 2007, p 57). In a variety of ways the New Labour governments sought to encourage practically and discursively the development of social enterprise solutions to 'wicked' or intractable social problems, and went some way towards establishing an infrastructure for social enterprise in relation to the public sector. For example:

- Working with Social Profit banks (Social Finance, Acumen, Bridges Ventures, Triodos) and the founding of charity banks (for example, UnLtd and Futurebuilders).
- Development of commissioning skills and forums (for example, Innovation Exchange).
- Support for and 'incubation'[6] of innovative public service ideas (for example, NESTA).
- Support for microfinance schemes and Social Impact Bonds.[7]
- Introduction of legislation for Community Interest Companies (CICs).[8]
- The Compact on Relations between Government and the Voluntary Sector, launched in 1998, is an agreement to improve relations between government and the voluntary sector to mutual advantage.
- The Social Enterprise Unit was initially established within the DTI and in 2006 became part of the newly created Office of the Third Sector, under the wing of the Cabinet Office. The Department for Health also had a Social Enterprise Unit and social enterprise fund.[9]
- A large number and wide array of social enterprise and for-profit providers were introduced in post-14 education and in post-compulsory education and provision for NEETs and welfare-to-work schemes. A public service market developed in response to what Fuller et al (2010, p 38) call 'the permissive social policy climate'; charity banks like UnLtd and Futurebuilders, and venture philanthropies like the PEF (see Chapter Five) and Impetus Trust provided support and financial investment for social enterprises and voluntary organisations to develop their work in this field.

Social enterprise and its relation to network governance and the deregulation/ flexibilisation of the public sector is now subject to a new iteration and reconfiguration within the Coalition's Big Society.

To repeat the point made in the previous chapter: 'Whilst the big society is presented as a new idea – and one legitimised in Cameron's early election campaign speech by reference to two left-of-centre US presidents, Obama and Kennedy – it is in many ways a development of welfare reform under Labour' (Smith, 2010, p 829). For example, the idea of Social Impact Bonds, which was floated under New Labour (see Peter Wheeler), has moved on to its first practical outing. In 2010 Social Finance created the first £5m bond in the context of resettling ex-offenders (www.socialfinance.org.uk/work/sibs/criminaljustice). Third sector organisations such as the St Giles Trust and the Ormiston Children and Families Trust[10] will provide intensive support to 3,000 short-term prisoners over a six-year period, both inside prison and after release, to help them resettle into the community (see Figure 3.5). Should the scheme be successful and repeat crime by ex-offenders be reduced, the investors will receive a pay-out of the savings made by the government on policing, prison costs, welfare and so on; should it fail, then the private investors carry the risk. The bank explains:

> Social Finance injects market principles into funding in a way that stands or falls on results – both social and financial. Our financial products forge essential links between the market, government and society for the greater good. (www. socialfinance.org.uk/about/vision)

Social Finance is committed to the development of what it calls a 'new social economy' based on principles of 'blended value'. This approach to problem solution and public sector reform rests on three premises of social enterprise:

1. A diversity of service providers;
2. A market discipline that rewards effective service providers;
3. Availability of investment to enable effective service providers to develop and grow.[11]

In August 2011 the Coalition announced a second Social Impact Bond initiative that would be focused on socially deprived families in four trial locations, with the hope of attracting investments up to £40m.

On a grander scale this is also the basic design of the Big Society and encapsulates David Cameron's vision of a new basis of funding for public service provision at a local level and is thus a means to extend the range of participants and types of provider.[12] Changes are being addressed on a number of fronts: the Cabinet Office is committed to 'Build the Big Society by promoting community empowerment, opening up public services and encourage social action'; the Office for Civil Society will develop programmes to enable capacity building for voluntary sector community organisers; it will provide start-up and transition funding for the voluntary sector – the Community First Fund and Transition Fund; the *Public Service Reform* White Paper (July 2011) outlines the methods of increasing the opportunity for voluntary sector organisations to bid for public service contracts, and signals the creation of Rights to Provide and allows public sector workers to take over the running of services;[13] in the *Plan for Growth* report, published in March 2011, the government also set out its aspiration of awarding 25% of government contracts to small and medium-size enterprises.

> The government's 'Open Public Services White Paper', due in July, will set out the bold blueprint for the reform of our public services. It is a process that is not just about efficiencies, cost savings or achieving value for money. But an opportunity to rethink and reform how services are designed, to systematically engage with communities and gain a better understanding of how to integrate services and create better outcomes. Releasing services from the grip of state control encourages bids for public work from voluntary groups, charities and the private sector. (events@ public-sector-events.org.uk)
>
> Each year the public sector spends around £220bn on goods and services. Now is the ideal time to sell to the public sector and take a share of that huge spend – this conference will tell you how.
>
> Our Win the Contract conference will help you through each stage of the process and explain how to make bid documents stand out from competitors. It is a must attend event for all suppliers interested in obtaining public sector business for the first time, those who have been unsuccessful so far and those who want to increase their business with the public sector. (events@public-sector-events.org.uk)

These reforms also aim to reduce 'unnecessary bureaucratic burdens', 'duplication and overspending'. Opening up public services to a range of providers is intended to increase competition to offer 'better services' tailored to 'local needs' and to allow for more 'innovative and flexible models' of provision. The government sees competition as crucial to raising the standards of quality.

Figure 3.5: Social enterprise

! People/organisations/programmes not discussed in the main text

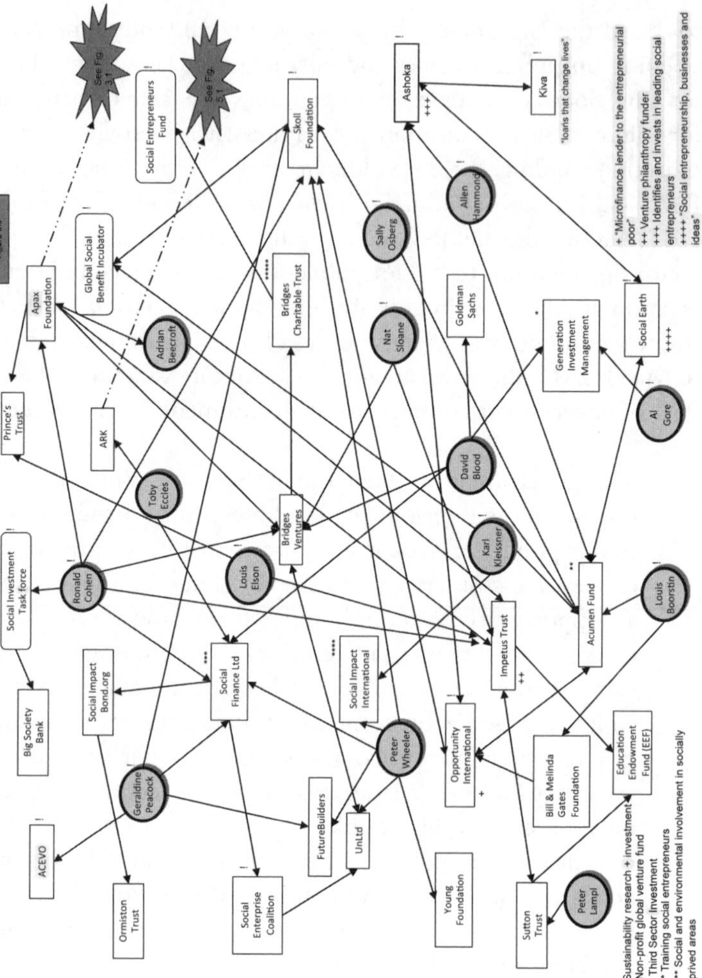

* Sustainability research + investment
** Non-profit global venture fund
*** Third Sector Investment
**** Training social entrepreneurs
***** Social and environmental involvement in socially
deprived areas

+ "Microfinance lender to the entrepreneurial poor"
++ Venture philanthropy funder
+++ Identifies and invests in leading social entrepreneurs
++++ "Social entrepreneurship, businesses and ideas"

Furthermore, drawing on Labour's 2009 consultation on the creation of a 'Social Investment Wholesale Bank', the Coalition aims to create the Big Society Bank, which will have a 'clear social mission' to catalyse the development of a sustainable 'social investment market'. The document *Growing the Social Investment Market: A Vision and Strategy* (Cabinet Office, 2011b) 'sets out the Government's vision of a thriving social investment market where social ventures can access the capital they need to grow, allowing them to do more to help build a bigger, stronger society. We also set out a strategy for achieving the vision, explaining how Government and others can act, including the key role of the Big Society Bank as a wholesale investor and champion of the market' (Cabinet Office, 2011b). This contributes a further crucial dimension to and move within network governance – the beginnings of a shift of some funding responsibilities from the state to the philanthropic and charity banking sector.

Assembling an alternative vision for education policy

Many of these sites and points of public sector innovation are joined up, as we have tried to illustrate, in well-integrated and complex social networks and discourse communities: taken together, they constitute a social assemblage of policy alternatives. This assemblage is diverse but has a certain coherence; it is emergent and dynamic, and is subject to re-assembly (in the transition from New Labour to the Coalition, the Third Way to the Big Society), but has certain qualities of a structure; it contains various authorities and forms of authority, and a variety of moral positions; it works through trust and social relationships. Rabinow (2003, p 17) has argued that assemblages 'are a distinctive type of experimental matrix of heterogeneous elements, techniques and concepts', which seems apt here. This assemblage articulates, advocates, tests and trials alternative visions of social and education policy and social services delivery based on a diverse but related set of principles that include mutualism, voluntarism, social enterprise and for-profit contracting-out. It operates in and across political parties, think-tanks, trusts, the corporate sector, charities and the voluntary sector and, importantly, now at points within the state sector, public services and higher education and with links to government departments and agencies. It has, in some cases, strong international links and it both imports (for example Swedish independent schools, US charter schools, SIFE, Achievers International, Global Leadership) and also exports policy ideas (for example Teach First, Partners in Leadership). People and ideas span between and move across these sites of articulation, so that in some cases the same people speak at different points in different roles.

The many disparate processes and varieties of actors within this assemblage of transformational impetuses are 'joined up' in various ways in networked social relations and an interrelated and cognate language of concepts and practices. That is, they make up a discursive formation – a certain regularity or unity between statements, objects, concepts, within the broad field in which knowledge is produced, embedded in a rule-governed set of material practices. The engine of knowledge here is not the individual actors but the discursive community that works to ensure that only some speakers are privileged and 'get heard' within the transformation of the public sector (Foucault, 1974, p 68). The sites and domains of the discourses effect the objects produced – enterprise, disadvantage and meritocracy – essentially a dual process of commodification and moral entrepreneurship (Shamir, 2008 p 2).

Here, what is privileged in particular is 'enterprise' writ small (enterprising learners and financial subjects) and large (Social Impact Bonds, Rights to Provide). As Rose (2007, p 19) puts it: 'The idea of enterprise links up a seductive ethics of the self, a powerful critique of contemporary institutional and political reality, and an apparently coherent design for the radical transformation of contemporary social arrangements.' In other words, the assemblage, through its co-functioning, symbolic elements (Thrift, 2005), brings to life a political imaginary that joins up changes in the form and modalities of the state with changes in the delivery and governance of the public services, with a reworking of the objects and subjects of education and social policy. That is, a new relation between government, business, philanthropy and the public sector.

Notes

[1] However, the Charities Aid Foundation 2007 Annual Report notes 'a fall in the proportion of high-level donors'.

[2] See, for example, www.philanthropycapital.org/publications/improving_the_sector/charity_analysis/Little_blue_book.aspx.

[3] www.teachfirst.org.uk/TFNews/TFPressRelease/CorpPressRelease_17647.aspx.

[4] www.sife.org/aboutsife/News/Documents/FINALGlobalImpactReport.pdf.

[5] www.businessdynamics.org.uk/gen/m1_i1_aboutus.aspx.

[6] http://archive.futurelab.org.uk/projects/informal-learning-ideas.

[7] A Social Impact Bond is a contract between a public sector body and Social Impact Bond investors, in which the former commits to pay for an improved social outcome. Investor funds are used to pay for a range of interventions to improve the social outcome. By enabling non-government investment to be utilised, Social Impact Bonds will lead to greater spending on preventative services. These interventions can have a direct impact on costly health and social problems.

[8] A CIC is a new type of company, introduced by the UK government in 2005 under the Companies (Audit, Investigations and Community Enterprise) Act 2004, designed for social enterprises that want to use their profits and assets for the public good.

[9] The Department of Health's Social Enterprise Unit worked with social enterprises to identify pathfinders that will lead the way in delivering innovative health and social care services. The learning from these pathfinders will be shared across the health and social care sector so that others can benefit from the pathfinders' experience.

[10] The Ormiston Trust is also an Academy sponsor and currently runs eight Academies and aims to establish several more. Alan Cleland, the chief executive, is an adviser to the NSN.

[11] www.socialfinance.org.uk/sites/default/files/Towards_A_New_Social_Economy_web.pdf.

[12] However, the idea and practical implementation of the Big Society are facing criticism on different fronts. On the one hand, its viability is questioned within public spending cuts that could significantly reduce the income of charities: 'established voluntary networks [are] threatened by spending cuts' (*Guardian*, 11 February 2011). Likewise, the recent report *Children and the Big Society*, launched in June 2011 by Conservative think-tank ResPublica, casts doubt 'about whether the government's localism and "big society" can succeed as public cuts bite' (*Guardian*, 18 June 2011). On the other hand, political analysts have pointed out the impoverished vision of citizenship embedded in the idea of the Big Society: 'The Prime Minister's vision of the active citizen as philanthropist and volunteer is a poor version of the real thing – the politically

literate citizen, knowledgeable about the major political issues of the day and actively involved, in different ways, in debates about how public or private services ought to be run' (Kisby, 2010, p 490). More broadly, analysts are also doubtful about the soundness and political sustainability of the project: 'Perhaps like New Labour's "third way", the "big society" will soon fade away or come in the future to be mentioned only with an accompanying snigger at its intellectual vacuity' (Kisby, 2010, p 490).

[13] This draws in part at least on the influence of Philip Blond, founder of Conservative think-tank ResPublica and the so-called Red Conservativism. In *The Ownership State* Blond (2009) argues for a new 'mutualism', that 'a new power of civil association be granted to all frontline service providers in the public sector. This power would allow the formation, under specific conditions, of new employee and community-owned 'civil companies' that would deliver the services previously monopolised by the state' (www.respublica.org.uk/item/The-Ownership-State-urtg-tbtp).

FOUR

Policy influence, boundary spanners and policy discourses

This chapter will return to some of the issues signalled in Chapter One as we attempt to visualise and actualise policy networks, to get inside them and examine how they work. As noted, one of the key issues in research on policy networks is the exercise and effects of 'influence'. That is, how do we map and specify relations of power in policy networks? How do we capture asymmetries of power within networks? This chapter will concentrate on the actors and interactions within and across a set of philanthropic networks and look at 'opportunities' within them for influence on the policy process. In particular we address the work of *boundary spanners* and the examples of the KPMG Foundation and the Every Child a Chance Trust in an attempt to explore the dynamics of networks, the 'networking'.

The chapter will also consider policy networks as discourse communities. Philanthropies and corporate philanthropies, in particular, are integrated in education policy networks and are being invited to work with government or agencies or in partnerships of various kinds in attempts to solve intractable and 'wicked' social and educational problems. Participation in these policy networks structures and enables the circulation of 'new' policy ideas, while at the same time working to simplify the policy process by limiting actions, problems and solutions. Such networks, as indicated in previous chapters, are part of a move, albeit halting and partial, towards a more interactive, fragmented and multi-dimensional form of policy making, involving the participation of a new mix of state and non-state actors. Across the terrain of education policy activity there is now a 'coexistence of multiple cross-cutting networks of varied length and durability' (Whatmore and Thorne, 1997, p 302), within which there is a recurrence of particular companies, organisations and people, related to particular kinds of education policies and discourses.

Multiple points of access, opportunities and their limits

As discussed in Chapter One, the central logic of the shift from government to governance is a reframing and rescaling of the state (Jessop, 2002) that involves a more interdependent, deconcentrated and flexible form of policy making (Stoker, 1998) done through network relations. There are two aspects to this: on the one hand, networks are made up of processes and relationships rather than constituting an obvious or fixed structure. Networks *are* a set of relationships – and we illustrate this in the interactions and activities of various network actors below. On the other hand, one of the effects of networks is an expansion of the 'territory of influence' (Mackenzie and Lucio, 2005) over policy, with the creation of new sites and 'opportunities' for influence on the policy process. The topology of policy is changed.

There are various possibilities of influence within policy available, in particular to corporate actors engaged in philanthropic educational programmes or sponsorship. These can involve the bringing of policy into being (for example, Teach First, see Chapter Five) or brokerage (such as with Every Child a Reader, which we examine below) or interventions into practice or problems (social disadvantage and achievement and literacy, for example SHINE on Saturdays) or supplementary service provision (extended schooling). All of these forms of involvement, in different ways, bring to bear and disseminate philanthropic discourses within policy conversations (see below). Corporate philanthropies are now directly engaged with government in educational programmes in various ways, including sponsorship, partnership, contracting and joint and matched funding. Alongside these is the representation of corporate interests on boards, committees, working groups, trusts and councils (for example National Council for Educational Excellence, National Education Business Taskforce, City Leaders Group, Mayor's Group, The Talent and Enterprise Workforce). Several of our research interviewees were members of these groups. Jim O'Neill attends the UK–India Roundtable (ministers and policy advisers also attend); Peter Wheeler was chair of Futurebuilders and sat on the Investment Advisory Committee of UnLtd; Gavyn Davies was the chairman of the BBC Board of Governors (2001–04); Harvey McGrath was the vice chair of the Mayor of London's Skills and Employment Board and chair of the London Development Agency; Anthony Salz was for some years a member of Business in the Community's Business Action on Homelessness Executive Forum and a member of its Education Leadership team, was also vice chairman of the BBC Board of Governors (2004–06), a co-chair of the Education and Employers Taskforce Trustees and has been recently appointed by Michael Gove as non-executive member of the Department for Education Board; Jean Gross is the government's Communication Champion; Peter Lampl and Lord Harris sit on the board of the Specialist Schools and Academies Trust; Amanda Spielman (see Chapter Five), research and development director of ARK schools, who is also a trustee of the New Schools Network, was recently a member of the Sykes review group commissioned by Michael Gove to review the school assessment system.

These various engagements (positions, memberships and relations with government, parties and politicians) offer a whole set of subtle but nonetheless important formal and informal opportunities to engage with politicians and policy makers. In a fairly representative way, one of the interviewees commented:

> "I know Ed Balls quite well and I know some of the research people, I know Nick [Pearce] who works in Number 10. So I've got to know them all. So, yeah, I chat with them about education issues but one or two others I know from this world that have, sort of, given up their jobs to be an education person full time."

Meetings and events in particular are occasions to speak to and establish relationships with ministers and officials: "… it was a good idea, it jived with Gordon Brown's 24/7 idea, so we had a big breakfast at Number 10, you know. I think even Fred Goodwin was there with sort of all kinds of accolades from the City." As with many of our interviewees, their spheres of work bring them into various forms of interaction with politicians (there were references in the interviews to breakfasts for city academies at Number 10 and several other instances of direct contact with state and government actors) as well as other major players in the business (mainly financial) sector. These are also opportunities for government to enrol business into the work of policy and its political projects. Yet in many cases these are social relations that are only partially visible to outsiders, and this complicates the task of network mapping and analysis. Social, business, philanthropic and political relationships are intertwined and interlayered, and function in relation to one another (see below). This means that what is important, what the limits of a network are and what the constituent relationships mean are hardly ever readily apparent or researchable. Promotion and voice, in particular, are extremely difficult to pin down, as they typically take place in private and can be glimpsed only indirectly. Indeed, by definition important aspects of network relations consist of informal social exchanges, negotiations and compromises that go on behind the scenes (witness, for example, the great deal of personal/'invisible' activity of Andrew Adonis, particularly in the early stages of the Academies Programme – "it was very much an Andrew Adonis thing", as one interviewee commented). Certainly it is the case that through the networks we offer in this book we can access only glimpses of influence, pale imitations of the real social interactions, the 'meetingness' (Urry, 2003) (see below) that ties people together in relationships and gets things done.

Nonetheless, it is clear from our data that business and social networks of various kinds do provide 'opportunities' for access and for advocacy that are well used. These engagements offer a wide variety of what Axhausen (2002) calls 'commitments/opportunities' to speak to government and speak about policy:

> "We were fortunate enough to have Jim, who was fortunate enough to get a meeting with the Secretary of State and he had some of his key policy people there. And we presented to them a pretty small selection of some of the work that we were doing and some of the work that we felt they might have been interested in. And then you just develop the relationship from there." (Stephen Shields, SHINE)

Positions and appointments also provide a set of links and connections accumulated over time that can be exploited for different purposes. As one interviewee commented: "I just got into a dialogue with officials … so we ended up in a partnership." Social events and encounters or other forms of 'business', as points of intersection between different social fields, also open up spaces and moments for social relationships to be developed. Some of these relationships provide very definite forms of social capital that can be deployed in philanthropic and policy efforts. In the networks football, for example, appears to play a particular role in building and consolidating informal social relationships and providing openings that can be followed up:

> "Gavyn Davies is an old friend of mine because of Southampton Football Club where he and I are both long-standing supporters.… And when Gavyn left and Jim succeeded him as the head economist within Goldman Sachs, I came to know Jim. With a common interest in education we bumped into each other from time to time.… And then he asked me to do it and I quite wanted

to, because of the subject matter as much as anything ..."
(SHINE trustee)

This is also illustrated in Jim O'Neill's long-standing support of Manchester United and personal relationship with Alex Ferguson, in turn a SHINE patron:

> "We've been very lucky with our patrons. And Sarah's [Sarah Brown, former PM's wife[1]] quite active, she's very good, as is Alex Ferguson. Fergie's been fantastic for us." (Jim O'Neill)

SHINE also sponsors the Watford FC youth team and the David Beckham Football Academy. David Beckham is a SHINE ambassador. Watford FC has a relationship with the Harefield Academy, fostered through the Academy sponsors, among whom are Michael Sherwood, co-chief executive of Goldman Sachs International, and Jonathan Green, ex-Goldman Sachs. Sherwood is also founder of the charity Greenhouse, which offers programmes in football, basketball, dance and the performing arts to socially deprived children (see Figure 3.1). West Bromwich Albion and Bristol City football clubs are also Academy sponsors. These interactions also relate to the role of celebrity in philanthropic activities (see below).

As noted already, some actors move around and across these networks in the form of network careers that cross the public, private and voluntary sectors, political divisions and types of role, as in the examples noted earlier. "He got involved with the City Leaders working group while he was still at the Office of the Third Sector" (Sophie Livingstone). As these actors move, they also accumulate significant volumes of 'network capital' (Urry, 2010). As Urry (2003) argues, 'because networked relationships are conducted at-a-distance ... seeing networks members face-to-face is crucial ... both to "establish" and to "cement" at least temporarily those weak ties' (p 161). As one of the interviewees commented: "I met with David Willetts this morning – we meet with politicians and policy makers, we're doing a lot of ... keeping in the loops." Being 'known' and knowing are important aspects of the functioning of networks. Some authors usefully distinguish between *network* and *networking*, arguing that:

> Networking denotes an action (a verb), a process that involves a number of actors and brings a dynamic relationship between and among the various actors of civil society ... Network is an identity while networking is a

process. Networking is much more than simple identity and is a continuous process (not future or past but present). While network pre-supposes coming together networking pre-supposes relating to (relates to somebody always). Networking becomes important to make network effective and impactful (Singh and Stevens, 2007, pp 4, 13–14).

Again as noted, the strengthening of trust is one of the most important possible outcomes of the 'work' of 'networking' and a central aspect of the interweaving of social, business, philanthropic and policy relations. Williams (2002) argues that 'trust is often isolated as one of the most important factors to influence the course of interorganizational relations' (p 111) and it is identified in particular as a key facet of the functioning of the financial services business (Rendtorff, 2008). This is what Granovetter (1985) calls the 'embeddedness' of economic action. Or as Coleman argues: 'It is legitimate to consider that trust reduces transaction costs within a network and trust therefore is believed to underpin network structure' (Coleman, 1990, cited in Christopoulos, 2008, p 477). In the research interviews there were numerous references to colleagues and associates in other businesses with whom new business ventures, philanthropic initiatives and activities in civic society were discussed and undertaken, for example, "Jon Aisbitt we recruited as a non-executive director at Man [The Man Group] when he retired from Goldman. I then recruited him to NPC as a trustee and a funder so, you know, these things do kind of build on themselves, I think" (Harvey McGrath). Peter Wheeler, Harvey McGrath, Gavyn Davies and Jon Aisbitt (among others), most ex-Goldman Sachs, were co-founders of New Philanthropy Capital,

> "They made quite a lot of money in the IPO Goldman Sachs and they wanted to give it away, or give some of it away, and they realised there was a problem in the charitable sector.... they wanted to invest in charities and there was no information." (John Copps)

This illustrates the interweaving of business/finance capital and philanthropy, and the financialisation of philanthropy – the 'growing and systematic power of finance and financial engineering' (Blackburn, 2006, p 39), as seen in Chapter Three. Furthermore, this is also illustrative again of the sociality of philanthropic networks, the joined-upness and embeddedness of the participants within the set of business relations and concomitant social relationships (social networks) that underpin the policy and philanthropic relationships.

Indeed, there is plenty of 'co-present interaction' (Urry, 2003, p 164) in the networks we have been describing. Philanthropy, in particular, is a highly 'social' world, marked by a constant round of social events, like dinners and awards. A very high-profile event is the ARK Annual Gala Dinner, which in 2011 raised £17.2m for the charity. Tony Blair was the evening's keynote speaker in 2008, London Mayor Boris Johnson addressed the 2009 dinner and Prince William was the 2011 speaker. The dinner is attended year after year by the 'rich and famous' (*Telegraph*, 7 July 2011) and receives significant attention in the press. *Hello* magazine (Issue 10, June 2011) dedicated a couple of glossy pages to the 'star-studded benefit' dinner where Jemima Kahn and Elizabeth Hurley were described as 'philanthropic beauties'. The £10,000 per head table that ARK founder Arpad Busson shared with the Duke and Duchess of Cambridge, among others, was reported on as 'an intriguing mix of the wealthy, the powerful and the beautiful' (*Daily Mail*, 11 June 2011). As mentioned by some of our interviewees, celebrity is significant in raising the profile of philanthropic activities and in generating donations, but celebrity also generates symbolic capital and points of access to other fields and networks (see Chapter Five). The SHINE benefit dinner is another highlight in the social calendar, 'stylish, sophisticated and oozing with atmosphere, SHINE's Benefit Dinners have earned a reputation for superb hospitality, top-notch production values and an attention to detail'.[2] Philanthropists like Jim O'Neill, SHINE's founder, bring to bear their financial and business skills, acumen and networking within charitable endeavours in a variety of ways:

> "... we do a big dinner every November and we're just coming up to it now ... I'm actively involved in trying to get sponsors ... I'm at the forefront of trying to get people to buy tables for a lot of money and get sponsors and ... And it weren't for being Jim O'Neill of the influential Goldman Sachs, I mean, I've been doing it so I don't know because a lot of these people are friends but ..." (Jim O'Neill)

Breeze (2007) suggests we have to understand 'giving' as a form of 'identity work', as something that confers identity on the giver and conveys symbolic messages that may involve promotion, recognition or rehabilitation. Indeed there is also a current proliferation of philanthropy and social enterprise awards and their concomitant award ceremonies where philanthropists and philanthropic activities gain recognition while at the same time ensuring the meetingness of these networks. There are several prize winners in our networks: Alec Reed has been awarded the 'Effective Giving, Overall Beacon Price 2010' – 'the top honour for philanthropists in the UK and described as the Nobel Prize of the charity world'.[3] Michael Spencer was awarded the Beacon Fellowship Prize in 2007 for setting up ICAP's Charity Day and Sir Tom Hunter was the Beacon Fellow 2003. Brett Wigdortz was named the 2007 UK Ernst & Young Social Entrepreneur of the Year and given the 2010 CASE (Council for the Advancement and Support of Education) European Leadership Award. Companies such as KPMG, UBS and Ernst & Young have all won the Lord Mayor's Award for corporate community involvement. The list of philanthropy awards is extensive; apart from the above-mentioned, there are SHINE awards, BitC awards for excellence, the BitC Corporate Responsibility Index, business charity awards (by Third Sector magazine and the Institute of Fundraising), The Charity Awards (sponsored in 2009 by Charities Aid Foundation and The Leadership Trust), and so on.

These sorts of social events provide opportunities for 'talk and touch', which produce and consolidate trust. There are also seminars, conferences, annual events, book and report launches, brainstorming sessions, policy debates and so on that serve both as spaces for networking as well as for presenting and discussing policy ideas. A couple of examples:

> "The main outcome of that [PEF's work with the City Leaders working group] at the moment is a conference that's taking place on 29 January and that's from 50 senior leaders from the three sectors, so third sector, government, business, coming together, with the morning session is looking at what's the situation, the background, the facts, the ministerial speech, the standard stuff. But the afternoon is going to be very much a working session on brainstorming different areas of the NEET issue." (Sophie Livingstone)

> "And this is where we invite about a hundred/a hundred and twenty head teachers from both state schools and independent schools […] And so it's an opportunity for them to network […] and a lot of them have actually formed partnerships and worked together outside and meet up outside the annual event." (Lorraine Thomas)

The Sutton Trust hosts regular seminars where policy makers are invited to participate in the presentation of research results or to join education policy debates. In June 2007 it hosted a session 'to examine the pros and cons of forming an independent Education Policy Committee to take responsibility for some key elements of education strategy and decision-making',[4] in a debate between Jim O'Neill (who had already presented his idea in a number of newspaper articles [*Financial Times* and *Guardian*, 24 July 2007]) and former Education Secretary David Blunkett, with Barry Sheerman, former chairman of the Education and Skills Select Committee, as a chair. The evaluation of the Sutton Trust's Reach for Excellence programme (a university access scheme for disadvantaged students) was launched in January 2010 at a seminar 'attended by university leaders, educationalists, access practitioners and policy makers'. David Willetts (Conservative Shadow Minister for Universities and Skills at the time) and Michael Arthur, chair of the Russell Group and vice chancellor of the University of Leeds, addressed the seminar. Indeed, attending 'around six events a year, including seminars and networking meetings' is one of the benefits that the Sutton Trust offers to its 23 current donors.[5]

The artful combination of moral and economic and social capitals can also ensure a 'hearing' within government for policy ideas. Sarah Brown is a trustee of SHINE, Cherie Blair was a guest of honour at the ICAP annual charity day in 2005, as were Prince Charles and Prince William in 2010. All of this gives a 'thickness' and a particular social texture to these networks, which are made up of a complex web of social and political and business relationships that join up finance capital with philanthropy, think-tanks and various bits of government and diverse politicians and political actors, across party divides, nationally and internationally.

However, in thinking about how these networks work and function, it is important to also recognise the limits to exchange and the lack of commitment within some parts of the state to the new governance narrative, as indicated in some of the interviews. This is an aspect of what Sbragia (2002) calls the 'two faces of the state'. One face, which is looking for new ways of opening up and deconcentrating decision making, represented by state actors who are invested in a process of 'market building' or 'state shrinking' – finding new ways to deliver services, provide solutions and solve problems through privatisation and contracting out and forms of social enterprise. The other face continues to be committed to older (or new) forms of centralised government, represented by actors who seek to defend and enhance the steering capacity of the core executive and who rely on more traditional policy narratives. Certainly, some of the respondents expressed their frustration with not being able to get their ideas across or not being able to get a clear commitment or consistent responses to their policy solutions from state actors. Two examples:

> "I sort of think very frustrating is that, I mean, we fund, I think, a lot of good research and we do a little bit ourselves, which sometimes affects policy. But essentially policy is determined by whoever happens to be in power at the time and the politics of the whole thing."

> "Unfortunately, I'd come to see how things are in government. The original sponsors and inspirers of the idea on a political level, and the administrative class who were frontline engaging with us, at a practical level, changed, you know, and much sight was lost of what this was originally about. And so the last two years became increasingly frustrating in that I think government forgot that it wanted to create something that had a certain amount of autonomy and that was going to be experimental and attack a particular issue, which was contracting between government and the voluntary sector and the public service by putting some commercially managed capital [to work]. And, you know, frankly that was very tedious and upsetting ... I don't think things are getting any better, in fact they sound like they're compounding the missed opportunities."

Despite all of this, it is important to recognise Parker's (2007, p 118) point that 'not all networks involving ties between actors can be regarded as serving a governance function'. Furthermore, Wilson (2003, p 335) distinguishes between multilevel governance and multilevel dialogue and suggests that the increased array of 'meetings' with government does not indicate decision-making influence. Indeed there are enormous difficulties involved in determining what counts as governance and where is begins and ends (see Bevir and Rhodes, 2006). This is also Pal's (1997) point when he says that 'This new situation will not completely overturn conventional policy instruments, of course, but they will have to be placed within the context of new assumptions' (see Chapter Six).

Actualising networks: the work of boundary spanners

Another way of getting into the complexity and elusiveness of the mobilisation of influence through network relations can be to focus on the role of nodal actors – the 'movers and shakers' (Williams, 2002) in a network, those with multiple and diverse positions within and across them. As Christopoulos (2008, p 3) argues, in any network, despite its size, 'not all ties can be assumed positive or reciprocated with the same intensity. In such a case the actors of interest are those who play brokerage roles or those who are most central within a particular cluster.' Burt (2001, p 6) also points to the significance of such actors and suggests that individuals whose relationships span 'structural holes' broker the flow of information between people who circulate in different flows of information and therefore 'offer inexpensive coordination relative to the bureaucratic alternative'. Similarly, Granovetter's argument of the 'strength of weak ties' (1973) suggests that it is 'through acquaintances [weak ties] that cliques are bridged and that information diffuses through a policy network' (Carpenter et al, 1998, in Peterson, 2003, p 14). Again, in a similar vein, Castells (2004, p 15) points out the significance of 'the controllers of the connecting points between various strategic networks; that is, the switchers'. These are a means through which power is exercised in contemporary network societies.

Nodes can be both organisations (for example Goldman Sachs, NPC, ARK and SHINE) and people. The latter are what Williams (2002) calls 'boundary-spanners', which he describes as the 'key agents managing within inter-organizational theatres' (2002, p 104). Some of the philanthropists in the networks presented here appear recurrently in a variety of roles and relationships, moving between fields and roles –'across boundaries' (Williams, 2002, p 107) – through engagement in multiple and complex positions that cut across the private, public and voluntary sectors. Here Harvey McGrath is a good example (see Figure 4.1), but there were some others among the interviewees who could serve as examples – and we refer to them briefly below.

Figure 4.1: Harvey McGrath

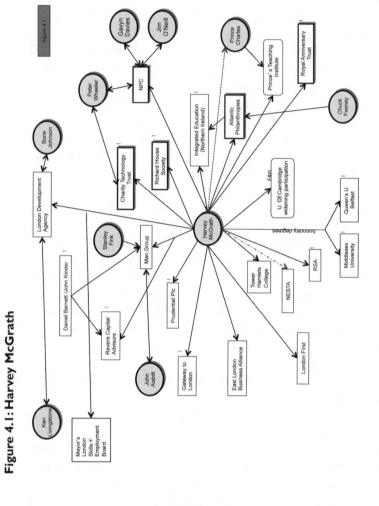

! People/organisations/programmes not discussed in the main text

McGrath has a background that includes work across a range of fields and sectors operating in business, philanthropy and quasi-public sector roles in a highly networked career, as nicely illustrated in this rather lengthy quote:

> "My journey is … I joined Man [The Man Group, investment bank] in 1980 but in New York and spent 10 years there – came back in 1990 to run the group in London, the headquarters. And Man was a founding member of what was called East London Partnership, which became East London Business Alliance, which is a business membership corporate social responsibility organisation focused on the communities in the East End, as the name suggests. So I became involved in the Tower Hamlets piece of that, which I chaired for five years, and then became chairman of the whole organisation. And, obviously, that was all about networks and so I learnt a lot about East London, Tower Hamlets, Hackney, Newham and so on. And that led me to become a governor at Tower Hamlets College because I wanted to do something which was grounded in, you know, I wanted some reality, if I could put it like that, not just to sit in an umbrella structure. The combination of Tower Hamlets College and ELBA [East London Business Alliance] and the local awareness of the issues of the communities there gave me a voice about East London, which was – which led me into government dialogue, both at the London level and at central government level, which in turn led me to being invited to join London First, which is not a charity but nor is it a for-profit organisation. It's a business lobby organisation, membership based, three hundred of London's largest employers. Which in turn enabled me to, sort of, leverage some of the things I'd been doing in the East London Business Alliance for the East End. And in turn, to cut a long story short, because of the London First role I had particular exposure to London government. I'm not politically aligned in any explicit sense. I became deputy chair of the schools and employment board under Ken Livingstone as chair. When Boris Johnson won the election he asked me if I would come in and be the interim chair of the LDA [London Development Agency], which built on all the things I just talked about. And, you know, the network effect of all that is, sort of, is self-evident …"

As Williams (2002, p 118) argues, by virtue of their position within inter-organisational networks, boundary-spanners benefit from 'being at the leading edge of information, having access to new ideas, gossip and happenings in other sectors, professions and organizations, and being able to seek support from and influence people in other organizations'. McGrath is clearly able to function and contribute in senior positions in different fields – financial, political, philanthropic and academic. As evident from his network trajectory, he is a paradigm example of Williams's *usual suspects* who operate within different partnerships – and who are important to making 'networked forms of governance' effective (2002). Through his work and other roles and networking activities, McGrath is a 'competent boundary spanner' (Williams, 2002, p 103) who has accumulated a significant volume of 'network capital' (Urry, 2010) and a concomitant fund of trust. McGrath appears to be a 'cultural broker' (Trevillion, 1991, cited in Williams, 2002, p 110) who can 'speak' different sectorial languages and is therefore able to link up sectors and bridge interests:

> "And so now I find myself with – taking the lessons that I've seen, not just from business but from voluntary organisations, schools, colleges in the East End, the effectiveness of corporate social responsibility programmes or otherwise [...] I think there is a lot of reward and satisfaction to be had from the contribution from bridging those, you know, the business world into the public sector and the third sector. And it's a sort of fascinating kind of nexus."

Yet the movement between fields is in part given its legitimacy, inasmuch that actors such as McGrath carry with them 'solutions' to 'wicked' problems. Indeed, boundary spanners are archetypal 'entrepreneurs', 'creatives' and 'rule-breakers' (Williams, 2002, p 110) who are willing to address in innovative ways those 'complex public policy problems [that] tend not to be amenable to tired traditional or conventional approaches'. At the same time that actors such as McGrath move between fields and sectors, they are contributing to a movement of ideas between fields, in particular, to a blurring between the fields and a convergence in their language and practices. The processes of translation of business into philanthropy and the parallel legitimation of philanthropic ideas and values within policy are examples. This is a venture capital model based on strategic funding and risk taking and the 'scaling up' of successful prototypes as discussed in Chapter Three.

Philanthropies seek to 'sell' policy ideas to government using outcomes evidence to make the case for wider take-up and funding (see below).

> "So what interested me about that is not so much narrowly getting people to the summer school [Prince of Wales' Teaching Institute] but what was the learning from that and how might that be scaled if you conclude that it has a positive impact on the quality of the teaching experience, you know, and so on and so forth. ... And I think creating some evidence base to demonstrate that, you know, this is an area that I think we ought to be concerned about." (Harvey McGrath)

Personal success in business and the association with successful businesses (as noted, many of the highly 'networked' philanthropists interviewed have a work background in successful financial institutions like Goldman Sachs, The Man Group, UBS, Standard Chartered and so on) appear to provide not just the financial means to engage in philanthropic activities but also the skills, legitimacy, authority and trust that make philanthropic and civic engagements more effective and a particular form of 'moral capital'. Sison (2003, p 31) defines moral capital 'as excellence of character, or the possession and practice of a host of virtues appropriate for a human being within a particular sociocultural context'. Or, in a word – integrity. Sison (2003) goes on to say: 'In business terms, good actions give us a return similar to what we earn in the simple interest accrued to money deposited in a bank. Habits are a payoff similar to compound interest, in which we receive a return not only on the sum deposited, but also on the accumulated interest payments made in the past.' Oddly, perhaps, the credibility of business 'success' does not seem to have been seriously undermined by the recent financial crisis.

Successful entrepreneurs and financiers have become contemporary cultural heroes, as represented in successful television series (for example *The Dragon's Den*, *The Apprentice*, *The Secret Millionaire*). So as well as linking up between different sorts of people and sectors, actors such as Harvey McGrath carry with them values, methods, discourses and practices that are not simply, as Bourdieu (2004) argues, forms of commitment, but also mechanisms of power – the right to be listened to. Indeed, by virtue of their positions and roles in business and their civic responsibilities, these actors have a unique and privileged access to the highest levels of policy activity and are able to become participants in policy conversations related to fields of interest far removed from their core expertise. For example, one respondent reported:

"Earlier this week, I was at a meeting with James Purnell [now working with Demos] and John Denham, two secretaries of state, talking about the integration of what DWP [Department for Work and Pensions] does and what DUIS [Department for Universities, Innovation and Skills] does in terms of getting people from worklessness into employment ... because of the work that I've been doing around the board, I know now people at ministerial level as well as at official level in those two departments ... I have used those contacts sparingly."

Again much of the networking activity of boundary spanners is 'invisible': it frequently occurs 'outside formal decision-making structures' (Williams, 2002, p 118), as noted, often through personal relationships, which is 'where interorganizational imperatives are translated into the organizational realities of individual participants' (p 118) and where social, business and political networks intertwine.

There are some other key actors in our networks, 'high profile' philanthropists (for example Jim O'Neill and Peter Wheeler in particular) who appear recurrently, moving between fields and roles – 'across boundaries' (Williams, 2002, p 107) – through engagement in multiple and complex positions that cut across the private, public and voluntary sectors (Boxes 4.1 and 4.2). Both Jim O'Neill and Peter Wheeler are members of a tightly interconnected, powerful and influential corporate elite. They have or have had senior management roles in leading financial institutions, in particular and significantly Goldman Sachs, and latterly Peter Wheeler in Standard Chartered Bank. Both are wealthy, both are very active within new philanthropy: Peter Wheeler was involved in founding and is a trustee of NPC (a research-based charity that gives advice and guidance to donors) and is also co-founder of the microfinance charity Impact International, to which he now devotes much of his time, Jim O'Neill is a founding trustee and the chairman of SHINE (see Chapter Three). As with Harvey McGrath, what is particularly interesting about these two actors is the extent to which they move between and operate across different but highly interrelated social fields – business, politics, philanthropy and the public sector. Both have or have had numerous roles and 'positions of possibility' (Harvey and Maclean, 2008, p 117) in these different fields and have accumulated numerous and significant social relationships within each.

Box 4.1: Jim O'Neill

Jim O'Neill was Head of Global Economic Research for Goldman Sachs from September 2001. In 2010 he became Chairman of Goldman Sachs Asset Management. He received his PhD in 1982 from the University of Surrey after graduating in Economics from Sheffield University in 1978.

After a brief spell with Bank of America in 1983, he joined International Treasury Management, a division of Marine Midland Bank. In 1988, he joined Swiss Bank Corporation (SBC) to start off a fixed income research group in London, helping to pioneer research on the ECU bond market. In 1991, he became Head of Research, globally for SBC. He joined Goldman Sachs in October 1995 as a Partner, Co-Head of Global Economics and Chief Currency Economist.

He is a board member of the Royal Economic Society in the UK. He is also on the board of the European think-tank Bruegel, and on the board of Itinera, a Belgian think-tank. He recently joined the UK–India Round Table. He is one of the founding trustees as well as currently Chairman of the London-based charity SHINE. He is also Chairman of Goldman Sachs European Charity Committee and a Trustee of PiggyBankKids. He also served as a non-executive director of Manchester United before it returned to private ownership in 2005. (www.ercouncil.org/jim_oneill.php)

Box 4.2: Peter Wheeler

Peter Wheeler is Chairman of IPValue and was one of the founders of the company in 2001 while working at iFormation Group, a joint investment vehicle of Goldman Sachs, General Atlantic Partners, and The Boston Consulting Group.

He spent 16 years with Goldman Sachs working in New York, Hong Kong, India, South Korea, Indonesia, Singapore and China, he became a partner in 1994 and returned to the UK in 1998.

He is an investor in, and a non-executive director of, Climate Change Capital and [was] a member of the Supervisory Board of Actis and the Chairman of Futurebuilders. He is a founder and Trustee of New Philanthropy Capital and Charity Technology Trust and was also on the Investment Advisory Committee of UnLtd. He is also a co-founder of Social Impact International, a social entrepreneur development programme, which launched its first project in Hyderabad, India, in 2006. He was Head of Wholesale Banking West, Standard Chartered Bank, between 2008 and 2010. (www.youngfoundation.org/about-us/people/trustees/peter-wheeler)

> "And I've actually found it, you know, Jim O'Neill of
> SHINE is not as good as Jim O'Neill of Goldman Sachs
> and SHINE, you know." (Jim O'Neill)

Both are extremely 'networked'. That is, they have accumulated formidable volumes of capitals relevant in these social fields – social, cultural, symbolic and economic. 'Capital represents power over the field ... the kinds of capital, like aces in a game of cards, are powers that define the chances of profit in a particular field...' (Bourdieu, 1985, p 724). In this case, the forms of capital acquired in one field are transposed into other fields – these boundary spanners are seen as 'policy entrepreneurs' (Williams, 2002, p 119) who can connect problems to solutions and mobilise resources and effort in search for successful outcomes and opening 'policy windows' (p 119). Jim O'Neill, for example, has written newspaper articles advocating the creation of an independent education policy committee to test and research education, the topic of debate in the 2007 Sutton Trust seminar referred to above:

> "I have actually written and published a couple of articles
> about education policy .... And so I went through a very
> active period of about twelve months around that trying
> to influence people."

Peter Wheeler, in particular through his work with Futurebuilders and as a leader of the City Leaders Group and involvement in the charity bank Social Finance, tried to achieve take-up by the New Labour government of the use of Social Impact Bonds to address major social problems:

> "That seemed to be a pretty good use of the global capital
> markets. One of those, you know, surely there must be
> other situations where these kind of problem-solving skills
> of people who work in this particular part of the business
> sector could be applied?"

In this process of transposition, the patterns of relevance in these other fields are altered. Networking and boundary spanning use up social energy, time and other resources. To a great extent, continuing effort depends on the extent of impact and effect of the movement of ideas between fields.

Different points of articulation, policy influence and new policy discourses

A further glimpse into the workings of influence in education policy and policy conversations through network relations comes from corporate philanthropy, in this case through the examples of KPMG and the Every Child a Chance (ECAC) Trust (see Figure 4.2). KPMG is one of the world's 'Big Four' professional services firms, employing over 140,000 people in a global network spanning over 140 countries. Composite revenues of KPMG's member firms in 2008 were US$22.7bn (14.5% growth from 2007). KPMG mainly works in three areas: audit services, tax services and advisory services. This includes financial advice, performance improvement and programme management to the UK Home Office, the Department of Health and the National Health Service. For example, in 1998 the School Teachers' Review Body commissioned KPMG Consulting to 'explore the key factors differentiating the roles of headteachers, deputies and other teachers with similar senior management responsibilities, and how jobs should be ranked, in a variety of school sizes, types and structures',[6] and in 2009 KPMG was commissioned by the Education and Employers Taskforce to 'look at the current state of school–employer partnerships'.[7]

KPMG is involved in a variety of aspects of education policy, and other policy conversations, occupying a range of roles and relationships within the state, and the educational state in particular, as sponsors and benefactors, contractors, consultants, advisers, service providers (see Ball, 2007, 2009 and 2011) and, indeed, engaging in a wide variety of CSR activities. KPMG sponsors the London City Academy, Hackney, jointly with the City of London Corporation. The school, opened in September 2009, has a specialism in business and financial services. This sponsorship operates through the Corporate Social Responsibility Division of the firm, which has other educational involvements. For example, KPMG was a founder of the Partners in Leadership national programme, working with the then NCSL (now the National College for Leadership of Schools and Children's Services) and BitC. This pairs a head teacher with a business leader, working together on the head teacher's agenda to discuss matters related to management and leadership. The programme was developed from a London pilot in 1996 initiated by KPMG. Mike Kelly of KPMG explained:

Figure 4.2: KPMG/Every Child a Chance Trust

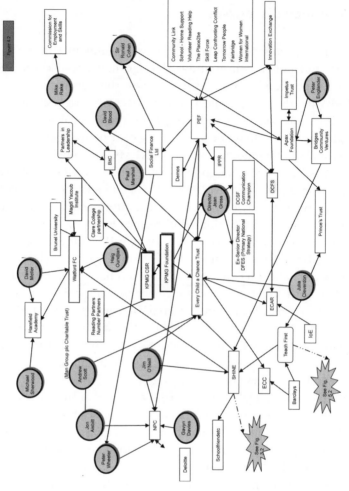

1 People/organisations/programmes not discussed in the main text.

"the senior partner for this office, at the time, went to a school and engaged with the school head there, talked about what issues she had to face. And, surprise, surprise, they were all the same sorts of issues that managers in KPMG have to face: business planning, HR [human resources], estate management, all the rest of it. So we ran a pilot programme for a year called KPMG Partners in Leadership. And had a group of twenty or thirty partners buddied up with head teachers to see if they could bring their skills to bear and help support that group ... So we made it a BitC branded programme just called Partners in Leadership and wrote up the manuals as to 'this is how to do it' type of work. Out of that we rolled it out around all the KPMG offices around the UK and then Business in the Community rolled it out to other businesses. And so it was one of those almost like viral marketing today, the way it grew. It has been very successful and you're talking, sort of, tens of thousands of mentors. It's spun off a lot of copy-cats, so there were social enterprise Partners in Leadership as well. There was a public sector piece where we had KPMG partners and other businesses linked in with senior people in the fire brigade, senior people in the police."

Since its launch, 5,000 head teachers have been matched with a business leader and 1,200 companies throughout the United Kingdom have been involved. KPMG also participated in the extension of this programme in Germany, together with companies like Herlitz, Deutsche Bank and Siemens. It provides mentoring support to head teachers in Berlin, Brandenburg and Frankfurt. The German scheme currently includes 180 schools.[8] A similar programme in Wales is backed by the Confederation of British Industry, Welsh Training and Enterprise Councils, the Education Business Partnership and the Welsh Office. KPMG has also worked with the National Workforce Remodelling team to develop the Financial Management in Schools programme (FMiS) and contributed a Financial Recovery Planning Checklist to NCSL's FMiS work. The FMiS programme was put together by a partnership of organisations – DfES [Department for Education and Skills], NCSL, KPMG, SHA [Secondary Headteachers Association], NAHT [National Association of Headteachers], NAGM [National Association of Governors and Managers], NGC [National Governors Council] and Confed [Confederation of Education and Childrens' Services Managers]. KPMG has been the NCSL's external auditor for some years and is currently the National College's internal auditor. KPMG has also worked with NCSL on a strategy to enhance the capacity of school leaders, 'including developing further the role of highly skilled school business managers that could save up to a third of headteachers' time' (NCSL announcement). This work has explored the potential of two new roles in primary schools – Advanced School Business Managers and School Business Directors – through demonstration projects in a range of scenarios. BitC, working with PricewaterhouseCoopers, KPMG and N.M. Rothschild and Sons, has delivered two of the demonstration projects focusing on secondary schools. It is possible to see these interventions and animation as embedding, in context-specific ways, the 'loose/tight' forms of organisational control that du Gay (2004, p 53) calls 'entrepreneurial governance' and 'the economic politics of enterprise', and as a key strategy for 'organisational reform in the public sector' (p 52). Michael Rake, former chairman of KPMG International (2002–07), chaired the UK Commission for Employment and Skills (2007–10). KPMG is also a supporter of Teach First in England.

Again, these initiatives and programmes offer multiple points of interface and engagement with and influence inside policy, they translate experience and 'responsibility' into effects in and on policy. Also as a 'partner', contractor and customer of a wide variety of state organisations and non-departmental public bodies, KPMG representatives are involved in events and meetings that provide opportunities to speak to policy. Again, these activities are part of the 'work' of networking and of network governance.

Like many other large corporations, KPMG also runs a volunteering scheme for employees to work with children in schools. KPMG also funds a Foundation, which was established in October 2001 and has a capital sum of £10m. The Foundation (a completely separate entity to KPMG LLP (UK) although totally funded by KPMG in the UK) focuses on 'education and social projects for the disadvantaged and underprivileged, with particular emphasis on unlocking the potential of children and young people'.[9] Most significantly, the Foundation was responsible for the launch of the ECAC Trust in 2007.

The ECAC Trust grew out of the Every Child a Reader project (ECAR), a three-year, £10m scheme (due to be rolled out nationally, in 2011 but whose funding by the Coalition government is now uncertain[10]) funded by a partnership of businesses and charitable trusts (including the KPMG Foundation, SHINE, the JJ Charitable Trust and The Man Group plc Charitable Trust with matched funding from the Labour government). The project was initially based at the Institute of

Education, University of London, and the involvement of the KPMG Foundation came about as a result of a long period of research that began with a concern with the issue of dyslexia:

> "Our starting-point was dyslexia but it led us to the larger issue of illiteracy. Learning that 35,000 children leave primary school unable to read and write was unacceptable to our trustees. Our research led us to Reading Recovery and from there we launched Every Child a Reader." (Jo Clunie)

The ECAC Trust also runs the Every Child Counts programme (ECC), which is aimed at Year 2 primary pupils who have fallen behind their peers and was again jointly funded by the Labour government. Barclays has signed on to be a national sponsor of ECC, pledging £1.2m, which will provide a coordinating structure to encourage local business to support at least 150 schools to help over 6,000 children aged 7 years who have the greatest difficulties with maths. It will also establish sponsorship relationships between 20 Barclays branches in England and their local primary schools. Businesses across the country are to be encouraged to contribute up to £12,000 a year each, over three years.

> "We are very conscious that every child needs basic numeracy skills for survival. That is why Barclays have committed to this national campaign in support of Every Child Counts. In the current complex financial climate, it makes economic sense to intervene early with youngsters to help them develop core numeracy skills which will help them manage their finances one day successfully, which in turn helps to drastically reduce the costs to society as detailed in this report." (Mike Amato, Head of Distribution and Product at Barclays)

In January 2009 the ECAC Trust published a report, *The Long Term Costs of Numeracy Difficulties* (Every Child a Chance Trust, 2009), which estimated these costs to be £2.4bn a year. The trustees of ECAC, in addition to Mike Amato, include John Griffith-Jones (KPMG chairman), Paul Marshall (co-founder of Marshall Wace Asset Management, a European equity hedge fund group with circa US$2bn under management and co-founder of ARK – see Chapter Five), Jim O'Neill (chairman of Goldman Sachs Asset Management and, as mentioned, co-founder of the charity SHINE), Dwight Poler (managing director of Bain Capital), Andrew Scott (trustee and deputy chairman of The Man Group plc Charitable Trust) and Corinne Goddijn-Vigreux (co-founder and managing director of TomTom NV, founder and chair of trustees of the Sofronie Foundation).

Companies like KPMG, through their senior executives and their whole range of social relations (as above), can provide fast and direct access to 'policy conversations' inside government:

> "We got that report onto Gordon Brown's desk a few days before the pre-budget when he was Chancellor and that was the turning point. He saw that and I think he understood the numbers." (Jo Clunie)

People like the ECAC trustees provide a very distinct profile for initiatives like ECAR and ECC, as well as delivering to philanthropic organisations established relationships with and within the state, and thus specific points of potential influence and access.

> "We have a great trustee who works for KPMG and understands how government works. We recognised that we had to build a coalition of funders to encourage government to support the programme at almost 50% of the cost. The total cost was £10m." (Jo Clunie)

Based on very direct points of access and relationships with state actors from which 'partnerships' are established, various kinds of flows between the sectors – of people, information and ideas, language, methods, values and culture – are opened up. Through schemes and initiatives such as ECAR, ECAC and ECC, from different points of articulation and in different ways, some of the methods and sensibilities of business and the narrative of enterprise are also imported into education. These corporate philanthropic interventions purport to offer innovative and joined-up responses to 'intractable social problems' that the public sector has 'failed' to solve and that are also politically attractive:

> "When we were running Every Child a Reader we thought about Every Child Counts and indeed came up with the title and vaguely talked about it to various politicians and officials. We'd hoped, this might be something we do next. But then there was a quite quick announcement by Downing Street; I think it was when Gordon Brown had just come into Downing Street at Number 10. We'd

worked with him in Number 11 before. There was an announcement that there would be a programme called Every Child Counts, it was a political announcement and I think nobody was quite certain then, including Downing Street, of who would run this or how it would happen." (Jean Gross)

In this case, a social problem is viewed from and to an extent constructed within a business perspective. Numeracy and literacy are seen as both educational problems and problems *for* business. Influence is being sought, and problems are being responded to, at local and national policy levels, articulated in this instance by a particular set of philanthropic discourses focused on problems of 'social disadvantage', meritocracy and opportunity (as illustrated in the focus of concern and activity of most of these charities such as The Sutton Trust, The Ogden Trust, ECAC, SHINE, and so on and discussed in Chapter Three), and related in very general terms to corporate interests (particularly evident, for example, through the ECC numeracy scheme, of which KPMG and Barclays are major sponsors). In a sense, corporate philanthropies are using outcome evidence to 'export' their policy solutions and ideas into government and make the case for wider take-up and funding. Reports like that on the costs of innumeracy also play a part in reframing the policy debate in ways that speak to the concerns of government and its policy agenda. Existing networks based on business and social and political relationships, with their 'embedded ties', are used and extended here – and in the process, trust and reciprocity are reinforced.

> "It is, you know, a conversation: the same sorts of KPMG people at the same level dealing with the same sorts of people at the same level in central government but having a conversation outside of the commercial world, yeah." (Mike Kelly)

Here again, meetings and events provide opportunities to 'speak to' and establish relationships with politicians:

> "When you do work in the semi-business sector you have tentacles there; through that to connections. And I have – one of the things I've learned is the business world operates to a much greater extent than the public sector on who you know and who your contacts are . . . Network, network, network. That was new to me, totally new." (Jean Gross)

Jean Gross, the director of ECAC, plays a key role in mediating and facilitating relationships here. She is another 'competent boundary spanner' (Williams, 2002, p 103), someone 'especially sensitive to and skilled in bridging interests, professions and organisations' (Webb, 1991, p 231). She has worked with local authorities, in consultancy, with the DCSF as part of Capita's National Strategies team and as the Communication Champion since October 2009:

> "I just got into dialogue with officials whom I'd worked with in the department and I think they thought about, well, who could do this and we could do it, the National Strategies could do it. And so we ended up as a partnership and we all do it, the National Strategies do it and we do it and officials do it, but I chair the delivery group. I try not to say that we run this programme. But we are regarded as the lead agency but not the lead funder, the government are putting more money in." (Jean Gross)

Another small-scale example of the sort of developments referred to above, where a new policy community is constructed operating outside of more traditional arenas of policy addressing the policy problem of NEETs was the Collaborating for Change conference organised by PEF in association with DCSF and Innovation Exchange (January 2009). The conference 'brought together leaders from business, charity and local government to forge new partnerships to tackle the NEET issue'.[11] As an outcome of the conference, a number of new areas of activity were opened up: an 'observatory' for good practice between the DCSF, Innovation Exchange and PEF; a NEET tracker (The Youth Tracker) collecting data relating to NEET, a joint initiative between PEF and the Institute for Public Policy Research; as well as a further workshop organised by NPC and Deloitte 'looking at metrics and measurement with third sector partners'. However, who was not at the conference is as significant as who was. Apart from a small number of local authority officers, attending as commissioners rather than as providers, no existing public sector interests were represented. As the new policy communities bring new kinds of actors into the policy process and enable new forms of policy influence and enactment, they concomitantly displace or marginalise more traditional public sector actors and agencies (for example local government, trade unions).

The PEF/DCSF collaboration around the NEET issue, on a small scale, as well as the KPMG example above, indicate not only the interrelatedness of participation in state education and policy conversations by philanthropic and private interests but also the blurring between the sectors and their interests, a blurring within which relationships and values are hybridised. In the next chapter, we continue to explore the hybridities, blurrings and crossings that are involved in the processes of network governance. We explore, in particular, blurrings involving some of the new 'hybrid' organisations that are emerging and evolving, and their roles and relationships in both policy development and articulation and innovative forms of service delivery.

Notes

[1] Sarah and Gordon Brown feature extensively on the SHINE website.

[2] www.shinetrust.org.uk/site/pages/178_benefitdinner.php.

[3] www.reedpressoffice.co.uk/newsArticle/Recruitment+entrepreneur+Alec +Reed+awarded+charity+'27Nobel+Prize'27/.

[4] www.shinetrust.org.uk/site/pages/43_news.php?pg=226.

[5] www.philanthropyuk.org/resources/philanthropy-directory/sutton-trust.

[6] See www.ntrp.org.uk/sites/all/documents/PSsummarypostFINAL.doc.

[7] See www.educationandemployers.org/media/6755/kpmg%20final.pdf.

[8] See KPMG's German website, www.kpmg.de/WerWirSind/10337.htm.

[9] www.kpmg.com/EU/en/WhoWeAre/CSR/Pages/TheKPMGFoundation. aspx.

[10] www.bbc.co.uk/news/education-11718968.

[11] http://privatequityfoundation.org/press/press-releases/collaborating-for-change/.

FIVE

New policy lions: ARK, Teach First and the New Schools Network

As noted in previous chapters, new philanthropies provided New Labour with opportunities for policy 'experiments' – new policy ideas, new ways of doing policy, introducing new policy actors. These new methods and several of the new actors are being taken up and taken further by the Coalition government – for example in legislation to allow for the creation of parent-led and so-called 'Free Schools'.

This chapter will address some of the sorts of 'new' actors, both organisations and people, involved in the processes of new governance and the relationships these have to the state and its project of self-transformation and the reform of the overall institutional architecture of the state and its scales of operation – what Castells (2000b, p 372) calls 'reprogramming'. It will focus specifically on three new policy organisations that have all been endorsed and/or funded by the Coalition government to grow and develop and take on public sector responsibilities and that are all involved in the new Coalition policy developments. It will look at the 'vision', 'interests' and relationships of these organisations and will discuss the hybridities, blurrings and crossings that are involved both in their roles and relationships with government and in the participation(s) of key actors. In doing so, the chapter will also give greater substance and specificity to the notion of network governance, conveying a sense of some of the relays, discourses, values, interests and commitments involved in governance activities and of how joined up, mutually dependent and reinforcing these new policy communities are. Some specific 'mobile' and 'hybrid' actors will also be profiled and discussed.

ARK: an ambitious philanthropy

ARK is a charity founded in 2002 by a group of hedge fund managers 'pooling their skills and resources to improve the life chances of children' (ARK website). ARK's activities are in the areas of health (in sub-Saharan Africa), child protection (Eastern Europe) and education (India, US and UK). In the UK, ARK is one of a number of organisations (charitable trusts, faith groups and social enterprises and businesses, for example E-Act, United Learning Trust, Harris Federation, Oasis Trust, Ormiston Trust and so on) that are running 'chains' of state schools as Academies and providing other services to education'.

Reflecting one of the dominant rationales and themes of the educational business foundations and charities (see Chapter Three), the discourse of opportunity and meritocracy is central to the work of ARK. The charity is concerned with educational disadvantage and seeks to close the achievement gap between children from advantaged and disadvantaged backgrounds. As Amanda Spielman, research and development director of ARK Schools, explains:

> "ARK has an overall purpose, which is to create chances in life for the most disadvantaged children. ... In education, having decided that we were going to apply that through the academies programme ... our aim is to make sure that everybody who comes through one of our schools by the age of 18 has real choices, either to go on to higher or further education or to take up a career of their choice that they're properly qualified for or eligible for the training."

ARK founder Arpad Busson (current member of the Global Board and chairman of ARK US), senior partner of EIM fund management company (with assets reported as ranging from £5bn to £10bn), described education as 'in crisis' and 'the biggest issue government face today' and argued that 'Charities must treat donors as if they were shareholders' (*Observer*, 29 May 2005). ARK's approach to charitable giving draws from the methods of the hedge fund industry. As a founding trustee, Paul Marshall considered ARK as an opportunity to create "a proper hedge fund charity, which demonstrated the commitment of the hedge fund industry to giving something back and which also used our combined financial and business experience to try and make a difference, apply some of the principles of our business to charitable giving" (Paul Marshall). ARK introduces its approach as 'venture philanthropy' (see Chapter Three) and describes it as 'a form of more engaged philanthropy which applied venture capital investment principles to the voluntary and community sector'.[1] *Enterprise* and the methods of business are seen as providing innovative and effective solutions to social and education policy problems of inequality and at the same time, as noted in Chapter Three, these methods are involved in reworking the modalities of philanthropy itself:

> ARK applies the same principles and disciplines to managing the Charity as it would to running a business. Programmes are therefore rigorously researched, piloted and assessed before launch, then monitored and rapidly taken to scale if successful.[2]

The argument is made that charities like ARK can be, as Amanda Spielman put it, "more flexible than governments about modifying and developing what they do ... start small and expand gradually and change what they're doing in response to early-stage feedback – a different sort of developmental model". There is also the claim that 'through its successful track record, ARK earns the right to a place in policy debates'.[3] Thus, ARK does not limit its ambitions to service provision but seeks to be a participant in the policy process. As we shall see, ARK is also keen to 'grow' its 'business' and to diversify.

The ARK board is made up of representatives of finance capital. Paul Dunning, who previous to establishing Finsbury Capital Advisers Pty Ltd, the hedge fund investments firm, was the founding CEO of HSBC Republic Investments Limited, is a director and trustee of ARK, as are Stanley Fink (recently made a peer), CEO of International Standard Asset Management and co-treasurer of the Conservative Party, previously of The Man Group (and who in 2009 replaced Arpad Busson as ARK chairman) and Jennifer Moses, former investment banker at Goldman Sachs (see also later). Another founding trustee of ARK, Paul Marshall, is co-founder and chairman of Marshall Wace LLP, a $15bn hedge fund, whose other founding partner, Ian Wace, is also the ARK's chairman. Paul Marshall also funds the LibDem think-thank CentreForum (see below). Paul Myners, recently appointed to the ARK board (November 2010), had a successful career in the investment management business (as chief executive and then chairman of pension fund manager Gartmore and as independent director of hedge fund GLG), before his appointment as Financial Services Secretary to the Treasury (City Minister) under Gordon Brown (2008–10), as well as leading government reviews under the last Labour government (*BBC News*, 27 February 2009). Here also, then, we can see the presence of 'boundary spanners', the relationships between business roles and policy influence, and the cross-party affiliation and involvements (of which more below).

ARK's main source of direct funding comes from fund-raising activities,[4] principally its very high-profile annual gala dinners – 'the annual hedge fund extravaganza' (*Telegraph*, 7 July 2010). These are attended by top financiers and celebrities and have raised over £150m since 2002. As noted in the previous chapters, the ARK gala dinners receive ample coverage in the press and have been reported as 'one of the most ostentatious shows of wealth in London's social calendar, with the highlight being a charity auction which one year raised £14 million' (*Telegraph*, 8 June 2011). As Stanley Fink commented, through philanthropy 'I get invited to places I'd never have seen otherwise', 'Give and ye shall meet celebs' (*Guardian*, 4 August 2008).

As of the beginning of 2102 ARK runs a chain of 11 Academies in London, Birmingham and Portsmouth and is expanding further, with eight more in development. Of the first 24 Free Schools opened in September 2011, two are primary Academies run by ARK (in North Hammersmith and Westminster) and eight more ARK Academies are planned to open between 2012 and 2013. ARK's approach to Academies draws heavily from US charter schools, particularly from the model of the Knowledge is Power Program (KIPP, see Box 5.1), as Paul Marshall explained in a newspaper interview:

> At ARK, we demonstrate that if you set high expectations, robust discipline and focus relentlessly on literacy and numeracy, poor children can achieve as well as prosperous ones. We model ourselves on the American KIPP schools that have 80 per cent on free school meals and send 80 per cent to university. (*London Evening Standard*, 7 March 2011)

Paul Marshall has also expressed his view that the only way for head teachers to reverse underperforming schools is if they "first of all sort behaviour". An emphasis on discipline and behaviour management is indeed among the central features of KIPP schools that have been visited by ARK Academies' leadership teams, for example Burlington Danes Academy (*Guardian*, 12 December 2006), sponsored by Stanley Fink through ARK Schools. In 2005 ARK hired Jay Altman, a 'pioneer of US charter schools'[5] and current chief executive of First Line Schools (a charter schools operator in New Orleans) as director for education. Altman has been a co-founder of the Future Leaders programme (see below) and has been promoting the deployment of non-traditional methods and actors in closing 'the attainment gap', as well as pointing to the heart of network governance when he claimed that 'a Government relying on a narrow spectrum of solutions has a much smaller chance of getting things right.' (*TES*, 1 February 2011). The Academies programme in general is a policy space in which experimental ideas can be 'tried out', and ARK in particular plays a significant role within that terrain. ARK Academies are being celebrated by the Coalition government for 'driving up standards in the poorest areas' and the Secretary of State for Education, Michael Gove, has indicated that ARK is among the Academy providers that represent the ideas he most admires in education (alongside Haberdashers' and Harris) (*TES*, 1 February 2011).

Box 5.1: The Knowledge is Power Program

KIPP is a network of charter schools (publicly funded/independently operated schools) currently running 99 schools throughout the US. Started by two Teach for America (see below) alumni in 1994, according to its website KIPP is now:

- A national network of free, open-enrollment, college-preparatory public schools with a track record of preparing students in under-served communities for success in college and in life.
- KIPP builds a partnership among parents, students, and teachers that puts learning first. By providing outstanding educators, more time in school learning, and a strong culture of achievement, KIPP is helping all students climb the mountain to and through college. (www.kipp.org/about-kipp)

However, a recent research report (Miron et al, 2011) linked the success of KIPP schools in raising attainment to the characteristics of student entrants, their higher funding (compared to traditional state schools) and high drop-out rates, concluding that:

> If KIPP wishes to maintain its status as an exemplar of private management of public schools, rather than a new effort to privatize public schools, it will need to convince policymakers and the public that it intends to recruit and serve a wider range of students and that it will be able to do so with sustainable levels of funding comparable to what other traditional public schools receive. (p 5)

Alongside government funding, KIPP schools receive funding from private donors and foundations through the KIPP Foundation and directly to the schools. The Doris & Donald Fisher Fund (co-founders of Gap Inc.) has been KIPP's leading supporter since 2000, alongside The Michael & Susan Dell Foundation (see Ball, 2012), The Robertson Foundation, Rainwater Charitable Foundation, The Bill & Melinda Gates Foundation, The Walton Family Foundation, The Goldman Sachs Foundation, Credit Suisse and a long list of others.

Richard Barth, CEO and President of the KIPP Foundation, was one of the founding members of Teach for America and is the husband of Teach for America founder and CEO Wendy Kopp. See Reckhow (2010) for an analysis of philanthropic funding of policy networks that takes a similar approach to our own.

In all of this there is a significant emphasis on leadership and the role of head teachers. Underlying the Coalition government's move to giving school leaders increasingly more freedoms is the conception that, as Michael Gove put it, 'The best schools share certain characteristics. They have a strong head and good discipline' (*Telegraph*, 2 September 2010). Huge expectations are vested in the role of school leaders, lone transformers of deficient schools, who are seen as bringing their vision and charisma to bear to raise standards and rescue poorly served students. These are embodied in the person of the hero innovator – Kevin Satchwell, William Atkinson and David Triggs are cases in point, as are Sir Michael Wilshaw, the head of ARK's Mossbourne Academy who replaced Jay Altman as ARK's education director (part-time) in 2008, and Dame Sharon Hollows (new head of ARK's Charter Academy, Portsmouth), honoured by New Labour for her services to school improvement. Mossbourne was among the first Academies to open and became New Labour's 'pride and joy' when, under Wilshaw's leadership, it was reported as having gone from being 'Britain's worst-performing school [to] one of the best' (*Telegraph*, 23 February 2011). Michael Gove is also a strong supporter and has hailed Wilshaw as a 'real hero', adding that he expected all schools to be like Mossbourne (*Guardian*, 5 January 2010). Wilshaw is also a trustee of the Prince's Teaching Institute, which is chaired by Harvey McGrath (see Chapter Four).

The emphasis on reforming leadership has been fermented and fostered by the work of the NCSL and the Future Leaders programme. The Future Leaders scheme represents another area of state activity in relation to education (alongside others such as the National Centre for Excellence in the Teaching of Mathematics [managed by Tribal], and the National Strategies [run by Capita] (now ended)) that is being contracted out to or run in partnership with private or charitable providers. The scheme was established in 2006 through a partnership between ARK, the NCSL and the SSAT: 'These organisations shared the vision for a programme to improve the life chances of pupils from disadvantaged backgrounds by raising their attainment through effective, inspirational school leadership.'[6]

Future Leaders is a three-year leadership development programme for current 'talented' teachers who have the potential to become senior leaders or head teachers of challenging schools, through an accelerated training programme. Participants are expected to 'gain senior leadership posts in challenging schools at the end of their residency year and will be working towards headship after a very intense four years'.[7] The programme draws again on the leadership model of US charter schools, which are visited by trainee Future Leaders as part of the international study tour section of the programme.[8] The scheme draws explicitly on business methods. These are new, fast-track routes with a slighter and speeded up experience of classroom and school life. These programmes stress loyalty to the programme and the sponsor and their values rather than to institutions, and play off career against commitment in new ways.

Again, Michael Gove has enthusiastically endorsed the scheme and has encouraged Future Leaders to look into setting up Free Schools: 'One of the best meetings I have had was on the Future Leaders programme ... They pleaded with me to go as fast as possible to change the Byzantine system we've inherited so that talented and enthusiastic teachers can start new schools in areas where people are not getting a fair deal' (Gove in *Telegraph*, 2 September 2010). This reflects Michael Gove's and the Coalition government's commitment to stripping out red-tape and bureaucracy from English education. Indeed Future Leaders now has plans to extend its work to involve Future Leaders in the setting up of new schools, thereby creating the possibility of a network of Future Leaders schools:

> To date, the scheme has been about getting this high-expectations culture into the state system by helping its graduates win leadership positions in existing schools. But proponents of the idea believe it is easier to achieve in new start-up schools, which is why the Future Leaders scheme is keen to exploit the free schools policy. The scheme will use the experience of its partner, the Ark academy chain, to give its graduates technical advice on setting up a school and is also looking at offering them a special six-month course. (*TES*, 16 July 2010)

One Future Leader, Peter Hyman – one-time speech writer to Tony Blair – has already indicated his interest in setting up a Free School. Here there is an interplay and interdependency between policy interactions within government and innovative 'energy' within the philanthropic sector – a kind of interactive policy process that is also bringing about governance changes. The landscape of state education is being reworked and traditional public sector provision is being worn away.

ARK also runs the Teaching Leaders scheme in partnership with the NCSL and Teach First. Paul Marshall of ARK has described it as Future Leaders'

"Next version, which instead of taking actual head teachers or potential head teachers, takes the younger generation, the kind of early thirties people, who will eventually be head teachers and fast-tracks them in a similar way. It allows them to go into model schools and to see what best practice looks like and then it speeds up their career path."

The scheme, set up in 2008, is a two-year programme that combines formal training, coaching and support to provide leadership and management skills for talented teachers to become middle leaders in urban schools. These new kinds of headship and leadership are also related to the development of new routes into leadership based on new forms of loyalty and sensibility – internal recruitment between Teach First, Future Leaders and Academies. For example, it is now increasingly common to find situations such as that of the Knights Academy, where there are six Teach First participants, two Teaching Leaders and two Future Leaders on the staff.[9]

Teaching Leaders claims on its website to have 'secured support across the political spectrum and from heads nationwide [...] to expand to urban schools across the UK during the next few years'.[10] Furthermore, both Future Leaders and Teaching Leaders have received the support of the Coalition government in the recent Schools White Paper:

> Third sector organisations including Teach First, Teaching Leaders and Future Leaders are helping to attract more of the best graduates and school leaders to working in disadvantaged schools [...] We will also support third sector organisations to expand the availability of their programmes. For example, Future Leaders is a three-year programme which is designed to support highly talented teachers to progress quickly to leadership positions in challenging schools. Teaching Leaders is a two-year programme designed to support the development of outstanding subject or middle leaders in challenging schools. We will continue to support both programmes. (Department for Education, 2010)

ARK has also developed the ARK Plus programme, an early-intervention centre for Year 7 pupils at risk of exclusion: 'ARK Plus is an innovative pilot programme which aims to support children whose disruptive behaviour and literacy problems make them most vulnerable to failure.'[11] The scheme consists of a six-months off-site programme at the ARK Plus inclusion centre, preceded by a six-/ eight-week period of work with schools for early detection of pupils with potential behavioural problems and followed by another six/ eight weeks of support throughout the re-insertion of the pupils into their mainstream school. During the pilot phase, up until 2010, ARK Plus recruited pupils from three London ARK Academies, but it aims to 'grow to serve other local authority schools'.[12] ARK Plus is an alternative to traditional local authority Pupil Referral Unit provision and is in line with the proposals of the 2008 *Back on Track* White Paper (Department for Children, Schools and Families, 2008) that 'a wider range of alternative education providers should step in earlier; so they can use their expertise to support mainstream schools more effectively'.[13] More recently, Michael Gove has expressed his intention to further diversify the range of organisations running pupil referral units, including not only 'city academies such as Ark schools' but also various voluntary groups, including one made up of army veterans (*Guardian*, 27 January 2011). It is claimed that: 'If successful, this programme [ARK Plus] should dramatically improve the prospects of children who might otherwise fail to cope.'[14]

ARK also ran for a time a two-year leadership training programme in India (School Leaders for India) based on the Future Leaders model, training 25 head teachers in Mumbai and Pune between 2008 and 2009. ARK India is now involved in two further initiatives, the ASPIRE (Allow Synthetic Phonics to Improve Results in English) programme to extend the use of synthetic phonics in the teaching of English in primary schools, and ENABLE (Ensure Access to Better Learning Experiences, in partnership with the Centre for Civil Society), a voucher scheme intended to improve access by the poorest families to schools in Shahdara (North–East and East Delhi). Amitav Virmani, ARK's Director of Programmes in India, was recently a lead speaker at the School Choice National Conference 2010: The Right to Education Act: Revolutionary, Redundant, or Regressive? run by the School Choice Campaign, which is a flagship project of the pro-market, Atlas Liberty Network think-tank, the Centre for Civil Society.

ARK therefore plays a significant role in the process of public sector transformation referred to in the earlier chapters whereby a variety of new organisations working in different relations to the state take up positions and roles previously reserved to the state itself and through which new practices and methods are brought to bear upon education problems, changing the way in which these problems are addressed. Some of the collaboration depicted in this section is represented in the network in Figure 5.1, which focuses specifically on ARK and NSN (see below) and the diversity of participations and sets of relations involved (as noted, to policy, finance capital, philanthropies and so on). Also this network joins at many points with the network in Figure 5.2 (below), where the focus is Teach First, again illustrating how well integrated these new policy communities are.

ARK also exemplifies the international movement of innovative ideas and innovation – 'borrowing', and the way in which new governance ideas and initiatives cluster – as 'discursive ensembles'. Philanthropy, social enterprise, forms of localism and 'market solutions' more generally are interrelated as alternatives to the traditional forms of public sector organisation and practice, with the effect of blurring the boundaries between sectors and producing a convergence of methods, sensibilities, values and forms of organisation.

Teach First: a transnational philanthropy

The network in Figure 5.2 centres on Teach First, an influential social enterprise that is deeply embedded between the communities of government and business and the complex 'post-political' social relationships now being mobilised around philanthropic solutions to educational problems. Teach First is a charity founded in 2002 and subsequently jointly funded by the government and corporate philanthropy, which again addresses a particular 'wicked' educational problem, as the website explains:

> Our mission is to address educational disadvantage by transforming exceptional graduates into effective, inspirational teachers and leaders in all fields.

> Teach First:
> Recruits, trains, places and supports 500–600 exceptional teachers per year who can make a real difference in the most challenged secondary schools throughout London, the North West, Yorkshire, and the East and West Midlands.
> Aims to build a new generation of leaders committed to advancing education, inside or outside of the classroom, through the Teach First Ambassador movement. (Teach First website)

Teach First (TF) is also an imported innovation, derived from the US Teach for America programme (see Box 5.2).

Figure 5.1: ARK and the New Schools Network

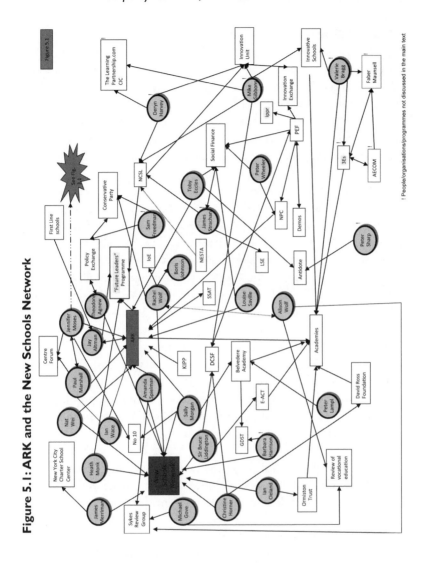

Box 5.2: Teach for America

Several TFA alumni have reached leadership positions in the education sector across the US: 'In Washington, [in 2008] TFA alums include the chancellor (Michelle Rhee), the deputy chancellor, two members of the school board, the mayor's adviser on education policy, and 10 percent of the principals' (www.slate.com/id/2175963/sidebar/2176234/). Ninety per cent of KIPP schools staff, as well as half of KIPP schools leaders, are TFA alumni. TFA founder Wendy Kopp was named by *Time* magazine one of the world's 100 most influential people in 2008.

TFA is part funded by the government at federal and state levels (for example, US Department of Education, New York City Department of Education) and by a large number of private and corporate sponsors, as with KIPP: the Doris & Donald Fisher Fund (founders of Gap Inc), Michael & Susan Dell Foundation, Rainwater Charitable Funds, The Walton Family Foundation, Bill & Melinda Gates Foundation, Robertson Foundation as well as The Eli and Edythe Broad Foundation (see Ball, 2012). Corporate sponsors include Gap Inc, Visa Inc and Wachovia among others.

Like ARK, TF has ambitions to contribute to policy. The chief executive, Brett Wigdortz, explained in an interview that TF is aiming to achieve both substantive and systemic change. That is, to bring new practices and new practitioners to bear upon education problems and to change the way these problems are addressed across the education system as a whole.

> "… it's really critical to get the best teachers into the most challenging schools, really support them to make as big an impact as possible and then long-term to create systemic change with our alumni group, our ambassadors. So it's really to get the most talented people to teach and lead in the most challenging schools and really support them to make as big an impact as possible."

Brett Wigdortz also captured the essence of network governance in describing the approach of TF: "We see ourselves collaborating with lots and lots of different organisations to change the world together, basically that's how we picture ourselves." Some of this collaboration is represented in the Teach First network (Figure 5.2) and the diversity of participations and sorts of relationships involved (to government, finance capital, schools, charities, social enterprise). Both the Labour and now the Coalition government have strongly endorsed the programme; as David Cameron put it, it is 'a programme that recognises our shared responsibility for raising standards in schools, combining business, the voluntary sector and schools themselves. Fast tracking exceptional graduates into challenging inner city schools is a great idea and one that should be expanded nationwide.'[15] The charity has received a new £4m government grant announced by Michael Gove soon after the 2010 election, which will allow its expansion to all of England and into primary schools. There is also a TF colleges programme.

Again, finance capital is heavily involved in the funding of the charity, with HSBC, Goldman Sachs, Canary Wharf Group, Barclays Capital and Credit Suisse among TF's major donors. The charity also has close relations with other education charities, for example, as noted already, with ARK, the Future Leaders programme (placing TF Ambassadors on the programme to develop their leadership skills) and Teaching Leaders, and is also supported by SHINE. Many TF students teach in Academies. Sally Coates, head teacher of ARK's Burlington Danes Academy, is quoted on TF's website saying: 'Teach First teachers are very enthusiastic, they're extremely committed, and they want to make a difference. They really want to learn and I've found them a tremendous asset,'[16] and elsewhere confirming: 'I recruited a lot of young teachers, a lot from the Teach First scheme, who were up for a challenge.'[17] Max Haimendorf, one of TF's Ambassadors (alumnus), became the youngest head teacher in England at the age of 29 when he was appointed Head of the ARK King Solomon Academy in London. Together with other TF Ambassadors, Haimendorf co-authored the *Lessons from the Front* (2007) report, a biannual publication by Policy First (funded by Credit Suisse), which, according to the TF website, 'enables ambassadors to influence education policy by: creating a forum for developing their views and recommendations; providing access to policy makers; and providing support in pursuing policy careers'.[18] Another publication by Policy First (supported by PwC) and written by TF Ambassadors, *Ethos and Culture in Schools in Challenging Circumstances*, came out in November 2010. The report identifies some elements that characterise positive school cultures and makes a series of recommendations such as that children spend more time at school, a practice that is already widespread in Academies. It was launched at the House of Commons and:

Figure 5.2: Teach First

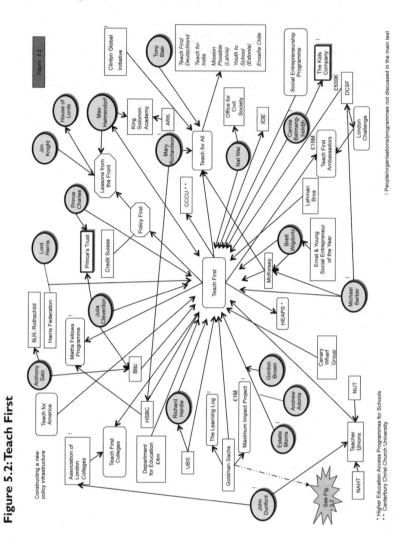

Figure 5.2

! People/organisations/programmes not discussed in the main text

* Higher Education Access Programmes for Schools
** Canterbury Christ Church University

… was hosted by Graham Stuart MP, Chair of the Education Select Committee. In his address to those gathered, he spoke of the credibility of Teach First Ambassadors and the valuable contribution they make to current debate around education policy. He referred to the fact that the editor of the report, Daisy Christodoulou, recently gave evidence to an Education Committee session exploring behaviour and discipline. Mr Stuart also highlighted the presence of Liberal Democrat, Labour and Conservative MPs and peers at the event as illustrative of the cross-party support enjoyed by Teach First.[19]

TF embodies the values and spirit of enterprise in a variety of ways and the lead actors embody the discourse of social enterprise and are emblematic of it. Through its Ambassador programme, it aims to promote this set of values. TF is perhaps a 'field builder' (see Ball, 2012), facilitating the interaction of and building of relationships, of a variety of kinds, with the state and in the private, public and voluntary sectors. There is also a strong resonance between the social enterprise methods of Teach First and the Conservative/Coalition idea of 'the Big Society' – indeed, in 2010 Nat Wei, one of the TF founders and a former McKinsey consultant, was elevated to the House of Lords and appointed as the government's chief adviser on the 'Big Society' in the Office for Civil Society. He is one of a number of hybrid, 'crossover' actors in this network (and see others below). Wei has been involved in the creation of the Future Leaders programme as chief strategist at ARK and is also the founder of The Shaftesbury Partnership, a social enterprise (Bartley, 2007, p 233) that in 2008 was commissioned by the Conservative Party to design a pilot for the National Citizen Service. In 2010 Wei was named by the *Evening Standard* as one of London's 1,000 most influential people. He was formerly a Fellow of the Young Foundation, a lead organisation for social innovation and entrepreneurship, which is chaired by Peter Wheeler (see Chapter Four), and is an Associate of Bridges Ventures, a venture capital company that specialises in investments with social and environmental benefits, and which is an off-shoot of Apax Holdings. Again, we see a philanthropic actor operating as a boundary spanner, and the interconnectivity of these policy networks and the embedded political relations of participants. Brett Wigdortz, TF's chief executive, is also a former consultant with McKinsey and was involved, together with London First and BitC, in the adaptation of the Teach for America model to the UK environment, work for which he was named UK Social Entrepreneur of the Year by Ernst & Young in 2007. He is a co-founder and board member of Teach For All. Wigdortz and Wei are networkers, network builders and social and policy entrepreneurs.

TF also claims on its website the 'enthusiastic' support of all the teachers' unions;[20] although more recently teachers unions' have become critical of the extension of TF into primary schools when 'teaching economics to a class of enthusiastic 16-year-olds is a very different proposition from dealing with the complex range of learning and emotional needs of a young child' (Christine Blower, General Secretary of the NUT) (*TES*, 9 October 2009). This is illustrative of both the dynamic and adaptive nature of these networks and the fragility of network relations, something also evident in the financial implications for the charity of the collapse of Lehman Brothers in 2008, although Lehman's commitments with TF were eventually made up by others (for example HSBC and Barclays). TF also has relationships with a number of universities that are contracted to do in-service programmes for TF teachers, including the Institute of Education, which delivers a custom-designed Masters programme.

Furthermore, TF, like some of the other philanthropic programmes, is now 'exporting' its methods and forms of engagement globally (Ball, 2010b). Together with Teach for America, it has created Teach for All, 'a global network of independent social enterprises that are working to expand educational opportunity in their nation by enlisting the most promising future leaders in the effort',[21] which is currently supporting initiatives in Brazil, Chile, Argentina, Israel, Lebanon, China, Germany, Estonia, Latvia, Lithuania, Bulgaria and Australia.

TF is growing and expanding in and over and against the public sector, working with organisations to which it is also a threat and a rival. It is an alternative to more traditional forms of public sector teacher education and is active in the process of public sector transformation and attrition referred to in the earlier chapters. TF is policy active, seeking to influence policy thinking and to 'scale up' its methods. Like the Academies programme, it is a policy space in which experimental ideas can be tested. The Coalition government's Schools White Paper 2010, *The Importance of Teaching* (Department for Education, 2010; see Ball, 2010a), indicated a move towards a more school-based model of teacher training with alternative entry routes into teaching, which seems to be modelled on the TF approach. Interactions and influence are in part celebrated in public through the website and newsletters, but also take place in private through interpersonal relations and via intermediaries. The senior executives of TF meet regularly with Department for Education officials. The relationships in the TF network are conduits for trust and for ideas. This network, like other governance networks, is tightly integrated in parts and more precariously and loosely integrated elsewhere (not all connections are possible to show in Figure 5.2). The already fuzzy divides between the public/state, the private and the third sectors are even more drastically blurred within network relations that are replete with ambiguity and hybridity.

Hybridities and blurrings: NSN and post-political governance

The last of our 'policy lion' case studies is the New Schools Network, an organisation that is closely associated with advocacy of and support for the development of 'Free schools' and that borrows loosely from both the Swedish model of free schools and US charter schools. The NSN is, according to its website, an independent charity that is 'helping 350 groups of parents and teachers set up schools, and introducing them to providers who can help turn their plans into a reality'[22] and is working with education businesses and Montessori and Steiner education groups.

The NSN was set up in 2009 by Rachel Wolf. Aged 24 at the time, Wolf had previously been an adviser to Michael Gove and Boris Johnson and is said to have had an input into the 2010 Conservative Party election manifesto. In October 2010 the Department for Education announced a £500k grant for NSN to liaise with and provide support to groups interested in setting up Free Schools. The grant has sparked controversy over the lack of accountability of NSN and the alleged independence of the charity. Both the fact that the funding has been given without tendering and that the charity's other sources of funding have not been made public (NSN does not reveal the names of anonymous donors) have raised suspicion[23]: 'The question remains why they felt that a lobbying organisation that was set up specifically to promote the benefits of free schools and has been in existence for less than a year was best placed to provide impartial information to groups seeking advice' (Lisa Nandy, Labour member of the House Commons Education Select Committee in the *Guardian*, 28 October 2010). The funding is significant, in the context of public spending cuts, and illustrates the increasingly complex crossings, blurrings, interweavings – hybridities – that constitute and animate the education terrain and its governance. Hence the remark of The Other Taxpayers' Alliance[24]: 'What strange political terrain we now inhabit: a state funded network the New Schools Network, promoting independent schools, and an independents network, the Local Schools

Network,[25] promoting state schools.'[26] Another example of the shift of responsibility from the state to philanthropy is the £110m Education Endowment Fund, established by the Coalition government in 2010, and based on Barack Obama's Race to the Top programme, which will be distributed among local authorities, academy sponsors, charities and 'other groups' to 'raise standards in underperforming schools'.[27] It is to be managed jointly by the Sutton Trust and the Impetus Trust.

The NSN has strong links with ARK and other Academy sponsors. The organisation has among its trustees Amanda Spielman, research and development director of ARK Schools, who was recently a member of the Sykes review group commissioned by Michael Gove to review the future of English qualifications and school assessment system, alongside ARK's education director and head of Mossbourne Academy, Sir Michael Wilshaw. It also has as a trustee Sir Bruce Liddington, director general of E-ACT, a multi-academy sponsor and formerly head of the Academies Division of DCSF and Schools Commissioner for England, and Ian Cleland, chief executive of the Ormiston Academies Trust, another multi-Academy sponsor. Heath Monk, one of NSN's advisers, is chief executive of Future Leaders and the former Deputy Schools Commissioner. Sally Morgan is another NSN adviser who is also an adviser to the ARK board. She is a former Director of Government Relations at 10 Downing Street and senior adviser to Tony Blair, as was Professor Julian Le Grand, also an NSN adviser. Baroness Morgan is also a governor of Belvedere School, a GDST school turned Academy that has been heavily supported by Peter Lampl, founder of the Sutton Trust. Also on the board of NSN is Theodore Agnew, a trustee of Policy Exchange, an influential conservative think-tank co-founded by Michael Gove (along with Nicholas Boles and Francis Maude). The NSN and Policy Exchange collaborated in publishing the report *Blocking the Best*, 'examining the changes required to make an expanded programme of genuinely independent state schools a reality', which pointed to the obstacles that local authorities present to new school providers. Another NSN trustee, Christine Homer, formerly part of Andrew Adonis's academy team is now working on the Havelock Academy as adviser to the David Ross Foundation. Toby Eccles, another NSN adviser, is a former UBS associate and head of research with ARK, and a non-executive director of Antidote, a charity developing emotional intelligence in schools. Toby Eccles is also development director of Social Finance, a charity bank founded by leading city financiers, including Peter Wheeler (who was also a co-founder of New Philanthropy Capital, and one-time chairman of FutureBuilders) and David Blood (who with Jim O'Neill was a co-founder of SHINE).

NSN also has international links, for example through its adviser James Merriman, CEO of the New York City Charter School Center, which serves as a resource and facilitator for new charter schools.

Following through these links and nodes are discourses of innovation, modernisation and social enterprise that stand in agonistic relation to traditional public sector organisations. Publications, programmes and events reiterate enterprise and autonomy as means of public sector reform. There are concomitant processes of destabilisation and destatalisation involved here.

A further link between NSN and ARK is through Paul Marshall, ARK schools' chairman and NSN adviser, who is also an advisor to the Liberal Democrats and a chairman (of the management committee) of the Liberal think-tank CentreForum. Marshall collaborated in writing a chapter in the book *Academies and the Future of State Education* (Astle and Ryan, 2008) advocating for the expansion of the Academies programme into 'failing' primary schools (*Telegraph*, 2 September 2010), the launch of which was attended by Michael Gove as Shadow Education Secretary (*Guardian*, 16 July 2008) and was reported as marking 'a fresh political consensus on academies bringing together Adonis, CentreForum which is closely linked to the Liberal Democrat leadership, and the Conservative party' (*Guardian*, 16 July 2008). Marshall also participated in writing the CentreForum publication *Aiming Higher: A Better Future for England's Schools* (Marshall, Moses et al, 2006), co-authored with Jennifer Moses, a trustee of ARK and ex-Goldman Sachs executive, formerly a special adviser to Prime Minister Gordon Brown and chief executive of CentreForum (2005–08). He also participated in writing the CentreForum report *Tackling Educational Inequality* in 2007, which:

> "Includes a proposal for a pupil premium, which both the Tories and the Lib Dems have now adopted as policy [in their manifestos]. And it also sets out an agenda for raising standards and expectations for disadvantaged children and models of how to educate them, which is very closely linked to what ARK is doing." (Paul Marshall)

A 'pupil premium' allocating extra cash for schools for poor pupils was announced following the Comprehensive Spending Review in October 2010 and has been introduced from April 2011. CentreForum and NSN also co-organised the conference School Reform: From Policy to Practice, held on 3 March 2010. Michael Gove (as shadow Education Secretary), James Merriman, Baroness Sally Morgan, Professor Le Grand, Lucy Heller, managing director of ARK schools, former News

International employee and partner of Professor Adrian Smith who led the highly critical 2004 report into post-14 maths teaching for New Labour (Marshall et al, 2006), and Liberal Democrat MP David Laws (among others) all spoke at the event.[28] Here we might infer the play of influence of various kinds, directly on ideas for policy, and the way in which new ideas once taken up by government expand the scope of participation of charities and social enterprises in service delivery.

New hybrid actors in education governance

In their current form the networks presented in this chapter have a clear Conservative inflection – nonetheless they still retain significant vestiges of their origins under New Labour through people like Bruce Liddington and Sally Morgan; Peter Lampl and Peter Wheeler have also had fairly strong connections to the Labour governments. Within all of this, there are now new kinds of actors and organisations in education policy and service delivery that constitute a new social enterprise elite or 'transform-ocracy' joined up in a complex web of philanthropic, political and business relationships that connect philanthropy with finance capital, think-tanks and various bits of government and diverse politicians, across party divides. As Clarke and Newman put it:

> Established typologies (the distinction between state and market or the hierarchy, markets and networks framework) fall short of new organisational forms and governance arrangements that are identified through such terms as boundary blurring or hybridity. Such terms mark the problem of naming these new arrangements, but bring problems of their own. (www.expanet-italia.net/conference2009/call-for-abstracts/18.php)

The new actors in the networks of new governance glimpsed in this chapter are migrating from business and bureaucracy and also constitute a new discourse or epistemic community (see Chapter Three), bringing with them new values, languages and practices. They are joined up around a set of themes and ideas which focus on social enterprise and the value of addressing social problems through social entrepreneurship and market solutions to supplement or displace state action. As noted in Chapter Four, these networks, as the ones presented in previous chapters, indicate again the production within policy networks of a new kind of mobile, hybrid actor and new, complex 'third-way careers', actors who move between sectors (state/third/business) and mix these in composite job portfolios. They are employees, consultants, trustees, with a variety of opportunities/interests/commitments that are difficult sometimes to pin down and unpack. Where the social ends and the enterprise begins is sometimes difficult to discern at organisational and individual levels. There are also various sub-texts and sub-levels to these networks and their embedded social relationships – the US and UK links (TF, ARK, KIPP, charter schools), the critiques of public schooling and educational reform in the US, the connections to News International (Lucy Heller, Joel Klein – see Chapter Two), to charity banking (Peter Wheeler, Toby Eccles, Social Finance) and the ubiquity of Goldman Sachs. Joel Klein said in a statement, 'I've long admired News Corporation's entrepreneurial spirit and Rupert Murdoch's fearless commitment to innovation. I am excited for the opportunity to be part of this team – and to have the chance to bring the same spirit of innovation to the burgeoning education marketplace.'[29] There is a weight, purpose and energy to all of this in the way that change is sought and influence is brought to bear at many points. There is also a very significant amount of new philanthropic money flowing through these networks.

The ambitious philanthropies and evolving policy networks we have addressed in this chapter are indicative of larger-scale changes in the landscape of social and educational policy that have taken place under New Labour and that are gathering pace under the Coalition government. These changes are not simply about who does what: they are also changing the forms and purposes and values of public service. These networks and the organisations and actors in them represent a formidable set of influences articulated around a very well-organised and shared discourse of reform and problem solutions. They constitute a highly developed – and developing – alternative infrastructure of policy and provision in education across a whole set of areas: teacher education and professional development, school management, curriculum and learning strategies development, school management, higher education access schemes, policy-related research, extended school programmes, work with NEETs and organisational development. When viewed together, these and the other examples we have presented both make a case for, and demonstrate the work of, network governance. We will consider that case more fully in the final chapter.

Notes

[1] www.arkonline.org/media/6762/ark_annualreview_2009__low_res_.pdf.

[2] www.arkonline.org/wp-content/media/30487/ark-director-marketing-comms-brief-feb-2011.pdf.

[3] www.arkonline.org/wp-content/media/30487/ark-director-marketing-comms-brief-feb-2011.pdf.

[4] The charity claims that further contributions have been leveraged through government grants (www.arkonline.org/about-us/our-approach).

[5] www.future-leaders.org.uk/news/2-archived-stories/13-tes-one-of-the-future-leaders-founders-jay-altman-talks-to-the-tes.

[6] www.future-leaders.org.uk/about-us/the-history.

[7] www.future-leaders.org.uk/our-programme/the-programme.

[8] *The Urban Leader*, Issue 8, Winter 2011 (available at: www.future-leaders.org.uk).

[9] http://gridreference.co.uk/index.php?/news/article/ofsted_results/.

[10] www.arkschools.org/pages/ark-schools/teaching-leaders-programme.php.

[11] www.arkonline.org/media/6762/ark_annualreview_2009__low_res_.pdf.

[12] www.arkschools.org/media/arkschools/Arrow/The-Arrow-Web%20issue%201.pdf.

[13] http://media.education.gov.uk/assets/files/pdf/t/taking%20back%20on%20track%20forward.pdf.

[14] www.arkonline.org/wp-content/media/6762/ark_annualreview_2009__low_res_.pdf.

[15] www.teachfirst.org.uk/OurSupport/oursupport.aspx (accessed 6 December 2010).

[16] http://graduates.teachfirst.org.uk/about/schools-pupils.html.

[17] www.edconnect.co.uk/2010/05/how-can-tough-schools-attract-teachers-3/.

[18] www.teachfirst.org.uk/TFNews/TeachFirstAmb ssadorsemployeesandguestsgathertogetherattheHouseofCommons16204.aspx.

[19] www.teachfirst.org.uk/TFNews/TeachFirstAmb ssadorsemployeesandguestsgathertogetherattheHouseofCommons16204.aspx.

[20] http://graduates.teachfirst.org.uk/about/index.html.

[21] http://teachforall.org/network.html.

[22] www.newschoolsnetwork.org/ourmission.html (accessed 15 February 2010).

[23] www.localschoolsnetwork.org.uk/2010/10/why-so-secretive-about-the-new-schools-network/.

[24] The Other Taxpayers' Alliance is an online campaign 'for fairer not lower taxes', set up in 2008 to scrutinise The Taxpayers' Alliance, and is run on a volunteer basis by ex-journalist Clifford Singer and bloggers (see http://taxpayersalliance.org/).

[25] An independent web-based initiative set up following the £500,000 Coalition government grant provided to the NSN in October 2010, to promote local state schools. The website has been created by a group of state education campaigners 'to correct the myths and lies that are spread about local state schools' (see www.localschoolsnetwork.org.uk/about-us/).

[26] www.localschoolsnetwork.org.uk/2010/10/why-so-secretive-about-the-new-schools-network/

[27] DfE press notice, 3 November 2010, available from http://education.gov.uk/inthenews/a0066416/new-endowment-fund-to-turn-around-weakest-schools-and-raise-starndards-for-disadvantaged-pupils.

[28] www.centreforum.org/index.php?option=com_content&view=article&id=187:school-reform-march-2010&catid=35:recent-events&Itemid=59.

[29] http://mediadecoder.blogs.nytimes.com/2010/11/09/news-corp-reels-in-a-top-educator/.

SIX

Networks, heterarchies and governance – and the beginning of the end of state education?

In this chapter we will draw together some of the main themes and issues addressed in the previous chapters and return to some key questions and difficulties signalled previously. In particular we seek to answer, or at least tackle, the very basic questions invested in the object of this analysis – network governance. That is, can we make a case for the shift from government to governance, at least in relation to education, and thus can we distinguish between networks and network governance (Parker, 2007, p 114)? Concomitantly, can we specify the work of network governance in relation to the examples presented? In other words, how does governance get done? Our research and analysis work has sought both to trace networks – their social morphology – and identify networking – the work within and of networks. Börzel (1997, p 1) says that that is what 'a theoretically ambitious policy network approach' must do. Crucially, as Parker suggests, 'in order for networks to be regarded as a form of governance they must play a role in steering, setting directions and influencing behaviour' (Parker, 2007, p 114). We believe that we have been able to offer plenty of evidence in our examples of all three (see below). Parker (p 115) goes on to elaborate the grounds for identifying 'networked governance' in Table 6.1.

Table 6.1: Parker's networked governance

Networks requiring
Actors connected by ties and social relations
Decentralised decision making involving shared power (absence of single-actor control and domination)
Information transfer and reflexivity (reflection on practice and world-views)
Actors participating out of recognition that they affect and are affected by the behaviour of other actors

Governance (decision making, steering, negotiation and coordination of activities) requiring
Density (direct or indirect linkages between all nodes)
Breadth (incorporation of full range of innovation institutions)
Trust, mutuality, common identity

Sharing, connectivity, reflexivity, density, breadth and trust are the key indicators here of functioning governance networks. We will discuss these and other factors in relation to the networks and social relations we have outlined. We will also return to the issue of the changing role and modalities of the state and changes in its steering capacity and think again about how 'new' all of this is. Finally, we argue here that a more nuanced and precise and analytically sophisticated representation of the specificities of network governance is offered by the concept of heterarchy.

Sharing, connectivity, reflexivity, density, breadth and trust

In the final analysis it is you, the reader, who must decide whether we have made a plausible case for network governance. Nonetheless, we would assert that the existence of new, dynamic and evolving policy networks has been made clear enough. We have, we believe, established that multifaceted, purposeful social relations now exist between the state and networks of non-state, non-public sector actors and organisations, focused on and addressing 'wicked' educational and social 'problems'. Furthermore, these networks are developing and enacting an expanding variety of policy experiments, initiatives and programmes, which are innovative and creative, as solutions to these problems, particularly those of social disadvantage, and standards. All of this is located within a more general process of public sector reform and modernisation – and the political projects of New Labour (the Third Way) and the Coalition (the Big Society). In some instances there are intimate interconnections between the politics of reform and network relations (Nat Wei, Rachel Wolf). There are a number of lead and link organisations (NSN, SSAT, TF) with steering and coordinating functions. The networks are self-organising and at least partly self-funding. These networks are interactive, kinetic and multidimensional (Rhodes, 1996). They are not static; rather, they are expanding and evolving. They are self-regulating, through consultation, coordination and partnerships, and through overlapping memberships (ARK, TF, NSN). Education policy is subject to, at least in part, what Harrison and Wood (1999) call 'manipulated emergence' – not so much a blueprint as an outcome of the interactions of participants, shaped by incentives designed by central government. We have indicated the sociality of these networks (dinners, awards, football) and the 'meetingness' of the participant actors – that is, the events, fora and activities in which they come together, based on a mutual recognition and common interests and concerns, and the keeping up of both strong and weak ties. These social relations are founded on commonly held values and attitudes and shared discourses based upon the virtues of enterprise and meritocracy. Generally, the discourse that animates their talk and that they enact engenders a belief in the generic efficacy of 'market solutions' to social problems – that is, enterprise in various forms. These are also moral fields that bind 'people into durable relations' (Rose, 1999, p 172). The participants are taking over both moral and practical service responsibilities from the state and bring moral positions to bear within policy making. The mutuality and trust on which they draw and which they reproduce are important here, and these rest upon extant social, political and business relations. Events and publications and websites indicate their common endeavours and shared concepts, purposes, intellectual points of reference and beliefs. There is a reiteration of principles and perspectives and key concepts through these media, and in references to 'thought leaders' and models of 'good practice'. The networks construct and use new 'information infrastructures' that 'interpret, frame, package and represent information about best practices ... and cutting edge ideas' (McCann, 2011, p 19). For the most part, the empirical-normative imaginary that is articulated with these networks is presented as a straightforward, technical, means–end, post-ideological position. In particular, we have emphasised and attended to the significant and growing importance of philanthropy within these networks and their values – both corporate and individual – we return to this below.

These networks have an evident density and connectivity, both a recurrence of actors and organisations in different roles and relationships, and high levels of interrelationship among the participants. Within these relationships there are some clear nodes and some notable boundary spanners, which hold them together and provide foci for information and mobilisation, and the communication of action and ideas between fields and sectors (for example McGrath, Wheeler, O'Neill). Nonetheless, they are diverse, and sometimes fragile, particularly at moments of interruption, like changes of government and financial crises. However, while some individuals and businesses withdraw, get disillusioned, move on, the networks continue and are becoming ever more firmly embedded within policy relations. In several cases the networks 'develop goals that override the goals of individual group members' (Parker, 2007, p 117). That is, they contain and reflect the work of ambitious members who are keen to take the opportunities of policy to expand the range of their activities. In this respect they display the characteristics of the business models upon which they draw in seeking to grow and diversify and increase their *turnover* and *market share*. Network here is no mere metaphor.

All of this is much more than 'a loose arrangement of social actors involved in talk' (Parker, 2007, p 117), although it is not easy to demonstrate the full extent of the connectivity and interconnectivity. Certainly the visual form of the network diagram and its practical limitations make it difficult to present all of the joining up and cross-integration that we have been able to identify. It is necessary to look across the different network diagrams we have presented, to see them alongside one another and overlaying each other in order to grasp their breadth and scope and the range of sites of influence to which they extend and the recurrence of key actors[1] The diagrams also fail to capture the generative and dynamic aspects of network change and evolution – they are snapshots that are out-of-date as you now see them.

The networks we have traced and explored include state agencies and departments and actors, quangos (NCSL), partnerships of various kinds, businesses, voluntary organisations, foundations and charities, social enterprises, community and faith groups and think-tanks. There is joint decision making between state and non-state actors (TF, ECAR, Academies, Future Leaders), funding and policy partnerships (NSN, ARK), and a continuity of cooperation (Teisman and Klijn, 2002). There is decision making influence on government in terms of scaling up experimental programmes (previous examples and Sutton Trust) and a wide variety of moments and opportunities of engagement in policy conversations. There is plenty of influence talk and activity, based on a lot of access to the decision-making sites of government – in the offices of politicians, civil servants and advisers, via advisory roles and places on advisory groups and in meetings, formal and informal, public and private, social and personal, planned and opportunistic. Particular actors within these networks take up formal decision-making or influence or coordinating roles (Harvey McGrath, Peter Wheeler, Nat Wei, David Triggs, Jennifer Moses, Amanda Spielman). The mobility of such actors through the networks and across traditional boundaries is also a form of cohesion and connectivity. In a social sense, these really are 'small worlds' (Urry, 2004). If we are able to establish the existence of an infrastructure of network governance a second interpretive problem remains. That is, to consider whether these relationships and responsibilities and the changes they signal also indicate and constitute a new form of state or are merely adaptations to the existing state form. Given all of the above, we argue that there is plenty of evidence of network governance at work, and that this is different and new. Clearly, it is possible to identify policy networks that existed prior to say 1990.

In education, from the 1950s to the 1980s, the relationships between the DfES, NUT and local authorities was a crucial component of the governance of education. Nonetheless, the form, extent, diversity and discursive distinctiveness of the policy networks we have identified are indicative of a different style of governance and a different form and modality of state work.

Network governance and the state

The argument we make, following Jessop and others, is that what is emerging here is a new hybrid form or mix of networks + bureaucracy + markets (Courpasson and Reed, 2004) that is nonetheless fashioned 'in the shadow of hierarchy' (Scharpf, 1994; Jessop, 1997, 2002; Whitehead, 2003). This new mix is realised in and through the modalities of 'metagovernance' (the design of markets, the reflexive redesign of organisations and the organisation of the conditions for heterarchies to self-organise – see Chapter Three) and also, cutting across these, through the interplay or dialectic of performance management and deconcentration. This is a potent combination that is conjoined in what we might call the *isomorphism of measurement*. The increasing use of performance management techniques by government sits neatly alongside the development of impact and effectiveness techniques within new philanthropy and by its infrastructural organisations (NPC) and the methods of business management. There is a proliferation of interconnected 'centres of calculation' that enable government to 'act at a distance' by assigning the responsibility for performance and its consequences to 'contracted' organisations and agencies that are both compared and combined. This is the means of 'governing through governance' (Bache, 2003, p 301) – the state becomes a contractor, performance monitor, benchmarker and target-setter, engaged in the management of 'the complexity, plurality and tangled hierarchies found in prevailing modes of coordination' (Jessop, 2002, p 243). However, this is not 'governing without government' – it is not a zero-sum scenario. Certainly in education the processes of deconcentration and destatalisation we have sketched are also accompanied by processes of centralisation. The new 'mix' involves changes in both the form and modalities of the state. Some forms of 'direct' control are being foregone (where they existed) in favour of 'effective' control through calibration and other steering mechanisms. Some parts of the state have less control than before, other parts have more – for example, where direct financial, contractual and administrative relations are established between the DCSF/DfE and schools and school providers, for example

Academies or school programmes (national strategies, ECAR, and so on). At the same time, local government, professional organisations and trade unions are increasingly marginalised and residualised. While steering may become more complicated across the 'tangled web' of policy networks, with the development of an increased reliance on 'self-administered' policy communities, the 'core executive' retains a substantial authoritative and coordinating presence within policy. Nonetheless, 'the state, although not impotent, is now dependent upon a vast array of state and non-state policy actors' (Marinetto, 2005, p 599). This is the challenge of 'governing the privatised state' (Hodge and Coghill, 2007) – a shift from 'directing bureaucracies' to 'managing networks'. As one senior servant quoted by Bevir and Rhodes (2003, p 185) puts it, central government is increasingly a space of 'synthesis' rather than of the 'design' of policy ideas. In some respects though, and certainly in some parts of education, the state has achieved an enhancement of 'capacity to project its influence and secure its objectives by mobilizing knowledge and power resources from influential non-governmental partners or stakeholders' (Jessop, 2002, p 199). This is not a 'hollowing out' of the state; rather, it is a new modality of state power, agency and social action and, indeed, a new form of state. That is, the achievement of political ends by different means. Also, we do not want to suggest that older, more direct methods of government and governing have been totally displaced (Dean, 2007) (see below), but there is great liquidity, intertwining, blurring and instability of powers in the processes of governance. The task here, as in relation to other contemporary social arenas, is to theorise continuity and change together. There is an important shift of *emphasis* involved (a new mix), but it is not an absolute break with or rupture from the previous state form: bureaucracies continue to be the vehicle for a great deal of state activity and the state does not hesitate to regulate or intervene, when it is able, when its interests or objectives are not being served. The process of governance through networks is increasingly significant but always contingent. This might be best understood through the appropriation of a term used by Tickly (2003, p 166), that is, what might be called here *governance-in-the-making*, which is comprised 'of complex and sometimes contradictory elements that provide both continuity and discontinuity [with] what went before'. What is happening in all of this is that states are 're-inventing themselves' (Mok, 2007, p 2) in order to successfully handle the challenges of globalisation.

Enterprise and morality

Philanthropy is one component within these changes and within the new mix of markets, hierarchies and networks, albeit thoroughly interconnected, functionally and through persons, with other components (state and business and social enterprise organisations and forms of public service). Philanthropy is a re-animated and resurgent mode of engagement in policy and service delivery, although also in itself much changed, and it is a significant contemporary form of policy influence and moral authority, among others, and an increasingly significant governance partner. Public sector education, philanthropy and business are increasingly blurred and increasingly convergent in relation to a 'foundational epistemology' (Shamir, 2008, p 14) – which is 'pragmatic entrepreneurialism'.

We noted earlier the importance of recognising network governance as a moral field, although, as Sanghera (2011) suggests, different modes of moral reflexivity are engaged (see also Moore, 2008) – arguably those he calls 'moral critics' are the key drivers here. Network governance is a moral field in a dual sense. There is a bottom-up morality expressed in forms of charitable giving and hands-on philanthropy and CSR – a taking on of responsibility for social problems – although Roberts (2003) suggests that CSR comes in different forms with different degrees of seriousness. There is also a top-down morality expressed and enacted both in the rhetorics of the Third Way and the Big Society – incitements to responsibility ('responsibilitisation' as Rose, 2000 calls it) for yourself and for others – in forms like volunteering, participation in local voluntary associations and mutualism. Thus, as an effect, the rhetoric says, social capital will be rebuilt and the 'broken society' (speech by David Cameron: 'Let's mend our broken society', 27 April 2010) repaired. These 'responsibilities' and social purpose and business reflexivity are complexly tied together within the virtues of enterprise expressed, in particular, through the methods of social enterprise and social capitalism. Morality and enterprise are also conjoined and realised in what Larner and Butler (2005, p 88) call the 'partnering state' – which is both neoliberal and neosocial; this is about both marketising and socialising the welfare state and the public sector, about both enterprise and relationships, competition and social contracting, 'doing well and doing good' (www.economist.com/node/2963247) in 'the new golden age of philanthropy'. These couplets signal the dissolution of the distinction between economy and society. As Shamir (2008, p 3) puts it 'there is a systematic market response to the "gaps" that had been left behind by the retreat of the neo-liberal state from assuming its socio-moral duties'. Together, these commitments and incitements constitute a very particular version of what Rose (1999), after Foucault, calls 'etho-politics' – drawing on and engendering civility, trust, community feelings, voluntary endeavour and 'engagement in the collective destiny in the interests of economic advancement, civic stability, even justice and happiness' (p 475). Self-government or mutual government replaces state government: 'etho-politics concerns itself with the self-techniques necessary for responsible self-government' (Rose, 1999, p 478). Government, or rather governance, acts upon 'the ethical formation and the ethical self management of individuals' (Rose, 1999, p 475) as individuals take on social responsibilities that were formerly the domain of the state – shifting 'the boundaries of responsibility between the state and the citizen' (Lister, 2011, p 74). In pragmatic political terms the link between the liberal and the social is to be found in so-called 'nudge' theory (Thaler and Sunstein, 2008). As Oliver Letwin (current Minister of State at the Cabinet Office) explained (Finlayson, 2008): 'we've been interested in "nudge economics" because it opens up new possibilities … [in] giving a gentle push to society to move in a direction of greater responsibility, or greater coherence, or more stability, or neighbourliness, or better health'. This approach is being addressed by the Cabinet Office 'Behaviour Insight Team', headed by former Blair adviser and social capital specialist David Halpern (see Ellison, 2011). Here citizen and consumer are articulated together in the trope – again initially developed under New Labour (see Ball and Exley, 2010) – of 'co-production' of welfare services, somewhere between the market and bureaucracy, within which philanthropy can thrive.[2] As noted already, we cannot think about this as a simple top-down process of change, as we have seen many of the philanthropies and philanthropic actors that we have identified are self-mobilising. These philanthropic actors are 'looking both ways' (Larner and Butler, 2005, p 94), to state and community – as well as being self-regarding.

Networks and governance

Given all of this, we contend that certainly in the field of education, policy networks do constitute a new form of governance, albeit not in a single and coherent form, and that they do also bring into play in the policy process new sources of authority, and thus contribute to the development of a 'market of authorities' (Shamir, 2008, p 10). That is, governance brings about and rests upon a 'diffusion' of authority at the same time as it privileges new sources of moral agency, in a variety of forms – corporate social responsibility, social citizenship, social enterprise and 'new' philanthropy. The modalities and contents of education policy and service delivery *are* changing, as part of what Burch (2009) calls 'the field effects' of new forms of participation. Nationally, in many different settings, the educational state *is* more congested as new and a wider variety of players 'enter' into forms of 'statework', bringing new policy discourses to bear and creating new conduits and means through which policy discourses enter policy thinking. The boundaries between state, economy and civil society *are* thus being blurred; there *is* a new mix within the matrix of governance involving 'complex relations of reciprocal interdependence' (Jessop, 2002, p 52). What is being established here is a more fully worked-up version of what Wolch (1990) called 'the shadow state', which is taking on more and more of the roles previously limited to public sector organisations and to the state itself, through involvements in delivery, dialogue and decision making. However, to reiterate Jessop's (2002) point, many of these changes and interventions are 'experimental' rather than definitive. These articulate, advocate, test and trial alternative visions of social and education policy and social services delivery, based on a diverse but related set of principles that include mutualism, voluntarism, social enterprise and for-profit contracting out. Not all of these experiments 'work', not all survive, but one of the clear advantages of the 'partnering state' is that the state can change its partners fairly easily – programmes and initiatives can be ended, contracts reassigned, agencies closed.

However, we want to consider also whether we need a somewhat different or more precise way of conceptualising these changes, something that goes beyond the 'Babylonian variety of policy network concepts' (Börzel, 1997, p 1) and brings them into a more coherent framework. We want to specify a set of dimensions, characteristics, relationships and functions that are embedded in new forms of governance, and the relations of power and actor roles that animate the work of governance, by outlining the concept of heterarchy. These are not 'just' networks (Parker, 2007); they are latent structures that are taking on an expanding and evolving range of policy tasks and public service delivery roles.

Heterarchies

Heterarchical relationships replace bureaucractic and administrative structures and relationships with a system of organisation replete with overlap, multiplicity, mixed ascendancy and divergent-but-coexistent patterns of relation. Heterarchy is an organisational form somewhere between hierarchy and network that draws upon diverse horizontal and vertical links that permit different elements of the policy process to cooperate (and/or compete). Heterarchies have many of the characteristics of 'assemblages' of and for policy and governance, inasmuch that they contain heterogeneous elements placed in diverse relations to one another, in latent structures or as a social morphology. Heterarchies are examples of what Kickert et al (1997) refer to as 'loosely-coupled weakly-tied multi-organisational sets'. They are sets of 'functions' and of co-functioning, symbiotic elements that are unalike but perhaps here also converging. They are temporary, compared with what they replace, and operate differently according to local circumstances, and may be relatively loose and opportunistic in parts – they are certainly uneven. They are made up of processes (exchanges) and relationships rather than constituting an administrative structure. There is a variety of asymmetrical and diverse power relations involved in this complex of reciprocal, multilevel, interdependencies, 'some happening spontaneously, others created deliberately through public policy and institutional engineering' (Davies, 2005, p 313), but overall, heterarchies are political constructs. They are nonetheless, to a varying extent, self-organising and, to an extent imaginative and experimental and, to an extent, polyvalent, and often involve considerable stumbling and blundering. They may thus be 'more likely to give bad decisions a second chance to be rectified' (Thrift, 2005, p 25), but equally, bad decisions may lead to the demise of elements or sections of a heterarchy. Various forms of power flow through the relationships and elements of heterarchies and are dispersed. New forms of power, authority and subjectivity are brought to bear through them in shaping governable domains and governable persons. New linkage devices and lead organisations are created over and against existing ones, excluding or circumventing but not always obliterating more traditional sites and voices. Heterarchies have porous boundaries, but nonetheless they also operate with rules of exclusivity. They are a policy device, a way of trying things out, getting things done, changing things and avoiding established public sector lobbies and interests. They are an attempt to 'routinise innovation' and incubate creative possibilities (Thrift, 2005, p 7).[3] They can serve to 'short-circuit' or displace existing policy blockages. As noted already, to achieve some kind of coherence and functionality these heterarchies rely on trust and reciprocity, and in some of their aspects they draw upon social relations established elsewhere, in business for example (see Ball, 2008b), or between charities, voluntary organisations and their lead and link organisations (Charities Aid Foundation, National Council of Voluntary Organisations, NPC and so on).

Within heterarchies, public sector organisations are positioned sometimes as clients, sometimes as contractors, sometimes as partners and sometimes as competitors of private sector organisations. In practice a great deal of the work done by the new 'public service businesses' (see Ball, 2007) is not done by taking services out of public sector control but rather, through collaborations of various kinds with the public sector, although some are more meaningfully collaborative than others and not all rest on shared objectives or a balance of influence. Partnerships also open up various kinds of flows between the sectors, of people, information and ideas, language, methods, values and culture: 'states have a key role in promoting innovative capacities, technical competence and technology transfer ... often involving extensive collaboration' (Jessop, 2002, p 121). Partnerships are a further aspect of the blurring between sectors. In these and other ways 'interests' and 'purposes' become increasingly unclear and difficult to 'trace' and pin down.

Within heterarchies policy making occurs 'in spaces parallel to and across state institutions and their jurisdictional boundaries' (Skelcher et al, 2004, p 3), and in the process parts of the state itself and some of its activities are privatised (Ball, 2009) or devolved to the 'shadow state'. The work of governance is increasingly dispersed and opaque (Clarke and Newman, 1997), being done in a myriad of policy microspaces 'tied together on the basis of alliance and the pursuit of economic and social outcomes' (Mackenzie and Lucio, 2005, p 500) – although the strength of such alliances should not be overstated. Heterarchies are indicative of a new 'architecture of regulation' based on interlocking relationships between disparate sites in and beyond the state and display many of the characteristics of what Richards and Smith (2002, pp 28–36) call a 'postmodern state', which is dependent, flexible, reflexive and diffuse but centrally steered. Relations here are complex but clearly asymmetric and they involve to some extent, in some cases, 'unnatural groupings' (Larner and Butler, 2005, p 81). Embedded here is a process that Shamir (2008, p 6) describes as a drive 'to distribute authority to numerous state and non-state units that assume the economic enterprise form ...'.

The relationships between the elements, as we have tried to stress, is diverse and unstable in a number of ways. The new cadre of 'heterarchical actors' is defined by mobility and hybridity. These actors, as we have tried to indicate, move between sectors, roles, values and sensibilities, and between national locations they are boundary spanners, networkers and 'field builders'. They are sometimes 'policy travellers' who 'spread' and 'borrow' policy. Their ideas move with them, they are 'policy entrepreneurs' who deploy 'intellectual ability, knowledge of policy matters, leadership and team-building skills, reputation and contacts, strategic ability, and tenacity' (Mintrom and Vergari, 1996, p 424) to get their ideas listened to and acted on. Policy entrepreneurs seek to construct and take advantage of 'policy windows' (Kingdon, 1995) and 'draw actors and policy communities together and align perceptions to formulate common goals and interests' (Oborn et al, 2011, p 340). They are persuasive story-tellers who are able to stabilise critiques, advocacy and flights of fancy into metadiscourses and logics. They are also flexible, 'knowing subjects' with a mix of new and old skills, adept in a variety of situated languages. Their allegiances, interests and purposes are sometimes difficult to specify (see also Greenaway et al, 2007 on the work of local policy entrepreneurs within the NHS). In looking at the 'work' of these actors it becomes clear that governance is a 'space of flows' (Castells, 2000b, p 412), an arena.

At the other end of these policies is, of course, the 'heterarchical worker', the flexible, 'modernised' teacher, learning assistant and support worker – another kind of new mix, in this case of skills, qualifications and pay. The 'modern' teacher will be less likely to be unionised, less likely to be employed within the framework of national pay and conditions agreements, and have less secure employment and be less likely to be qualified at all – Free Schools are free to employ unqualified teachers. What MacKinnon (2000) calls the 'enclosures' of professional expertise are thoroughly breached. The heterarchical worker is also being made up as a 'performing' and enterprising subject who is continuously measured and compared, judged and reviewed – another facet of the *isomorphism of performance*.

Government, governance and the 'end' of state education

As indicated already, the changes we are describing here are situated in relation to a broader set of practical techniques of government that have in part the aim and effect of producing new kinds of 'active' and responsible, entrepreneurial citizens and workers – indeed there is an explosion in modes of governing of this sort. As Triantafillou (2004b, p 11) suggests, 'we could broadly characterize network governance as the diverse governmental rationalities, technologies and norms that seek to govern by promoting the self-steering capacities of individuals and organisations'. However, to reiterate, this is only a partial description of contemporary government. In thinking about these strategies and technologies that are involved in what is sometimes called 'creative government', *it is new kinds of mixes, different blends of steering and rowing, that are enacted.* Various kinds of sovereign power and violence are very much still with us. Indeed, 'there is a contemporary proliferation of the techniques of arrest, incarceration, punishment, expulsion, disqualification and more broadly coercion ...' (Dean, 2007). These are indicative of what Jessop (2002, p 201) calls 'countertrends in the state', drawing on Poulantzas' notion of 'conservation-dissolution' effects. Such effects 'exist insofar as past forms and functions of the state are conserved and/or dissolved as the state is transformed' (Jessop, 2002, p 201). Thus, alongside the use of new techniques of governing that rely upon the 'conduct of conduct', existing methods based upon the sovereign and bio-political powers of life and death remain firmly in place and new ones are being invented. The point is that we should not expect or look for a consistency between sovereign forms of government and governmentality, nor should we be surprised by failures of government: the mixes involved are sometimes unstable. The particular form of hybridity of government in any setting requires empirical mapping – 'the state cannot be used to explain events but must itself be explained through empirical analysis' (MacKinnon, 2000).

Altogether, four sorts of related changes are going on here. One is in forms of government (its systems and structures), another in the form and type of the participants in processes of governance, a third in the prevailing discourses that flow within and articulate governance, and a fourth in the governing and production of new kinds of 'willing' subjects. To reiterate for the last time: 'This new situation does not completely overturn conventional policy instruments, of course, but they will have to be placed within the context of new assumptions – a new regime' (Pal, 1997, p 5) – a new dispositif. Thus, Jessop suggests that what he calls 'the nightwatchman state' is 'rarely strong enough to resist pressures to intervene when anticipated political advantage is at stake' (2002 p 243). Indeed, he goes on to say, attempts at coordination are always 'incomplete' (p 244) and always likely to fail. In order to continue, regimes of metagovernance require a degree of self-reflexive 'irony', that is, an ability to 'recognize the likelihood of failure but proceed as if success were possible' (p 245). As Grimaldi (2011, p 146) puts it, we need to be wary of 'the ingenuous optimism showed by the champions of the discourse on networks'.

In this book we have offered a glimpse into the increasingly complex, differentiated and opaque relationships of educational network governance and we have sought to illustrate and explain the interrelatedness of participation in state education, education discourses and education policy conversations by philanthropic, voluntary and private interests (both organisations and individuals), as well as to indicate the blurring between these. Within the processes of the modernisation and transformation of the public sector, the boundaries and spatial horizons and flows of influence and engagement around education are being stretched, dispersed and reconfigured in a whole variety of ways. However, networks are made up of holes as well as connections, they mix localism with innovation and diversity to produce 'patchworks' of practice and provision. As a result, the structural and architectural landscape of education provision is being redrawn and rebuilt (literally). It may well be that the sum of these changes marks a major turning-point in English educational history, in effect the beginning of the end of state education in its 'welfare' form. This is a second liberalism, a decisive move from a system of state education to a system of state-funded education networks; the return to the patchwork of provision and providers, somewhat like that pre-1870, accompanied by a return to traditional methods and the 'basics' (see Hatcher, 2011). This is a form of creative destruction, several things are happening together: destatalisation and deconcentration, centralisation and flexibilisation. Both the form and methods of public service provision are changing and state education is being disarticulated. On the one hand, one consequence and casualty of all of this is the role of local democracy in educational decision making and planning (see Hatcher, 2012) – that is, 'democratic deficit'. As Greenaway et al (2007, p 736) put it: 'networks can reduce the need for open democratic debate', and as Sullivan (2003) notes, traditional norms of accountability are weakened in a policy environment of 'many hands' and individualised action or, as Sørensen and Torfing (2008) put it, a system of governance that is primarily interpersonal has a weak 'democratic anchorage'. As we have seen, wealth and particular social and moral capitals offer privileged access to influence and control in the emerging regime of heterarchical governance. On the other hand, at the same time, there is an opening up of *some* new opportunities for some local, grassroots activity. This is a further ambiguity and polyvalency in network governance: 'As forms of coordination, networks actually have the potential to sustain and promote participatory processes ... At the same time, networks can work as a dispositif to hierarchically transfer contents and practices planned by experts, technocrats, governments and interest groups' (Grimaldi, 2011, p 147). We may also be seeing the construction of an infrastructure, legal, relational and discursive, that creates the possibility for further policy 'moves'. Specifically, 'moves' towards the large-scale participation of private providers running chains of schools (as in Sweden and the US) and institutions of further and higher education, alongside charities, faith groups, mutuals, foundations, parents and voluntary and community associations.

Notes

[1] If we had been able to use appropriate quantitative analysis techniques we might have been able to demonstrate this density in other ways, but the materials did not lend themselves to such an approach, involving as they do a blend of 'whole networks' and 'ego networks' (Knox, Savage and Harvey, 2006, p 118), nor do we have appropriate benchmarks and comparators. Also, as we note, these are evolving and generative networks with changing boundaries, 'poised between order and randomness' (Watts, 1999), and are thus difficult to capture, analyse and represent.

[2] Although at the same time spending cuts could reduce income to charities from government sources by between £4bn and 5bn.

[3] However, a recent OECD report (Lubienski, 2009, p 27) concluded that 'exhaustive studies in the UK quasi-market find little evidence of academic innovations, despite this being an explicit policy objective ...'. Rather, the report concludes that quasi-markets produce traditional teaching methods and standardisation.

Research interviews

- Jon Aisbitt (New Philanthropy Capital; Goldman Sachs; The Man Group)
- Adrian Beecroft (Apax Partners)
- Peter Bull (HSBC Global Education Trust)
- Jo Clunie (KPMG Foundation)
- John Copps (New Philanthropy Capital)
- John Craig (Innovation Exchange Director)
- Peter Englander (Apax Foundation)
- Charlie Green (Private Equity Foundation; Candover Equity)
- Jean Gross (Every Child a Chance)
- Richard Hardie (UBS)
- Mike Kelly (KPMG)
- Peter Lampl (Sutton Trust)
- Sophie Livingstone (Private Equity Foundation)
- Harris Lord (Harris Federation)
- Paul Marshall (ARK; Marshall Wace LLP)
- Harvey McGrath (New Philanthropy Capital)
- Jim O'Neill (SHINE; Goldman Sachs)
- Peter Ogden (Ogden Trust)
- Alec Reed (Reed Foundation; The Big Give)
- Anthony Salz (N.M. Rothschild)
- Stephen Shields (SHINE)
- Amanda Spielman (ARK)
- Lorraine Thomas (HSBC Global Education Trust)
- Peter Wheeler (New Philanthropy Capital; Social Impact International; Standard Chartered)
- Brett Wigdortz (Teach First)

References

Agranoff, R. (2003). *A new look at the value-adding functions of intergovernmental networks.* 7th National Public Management Research Conference, Georgetown University.

Agranoff, R. and M. Maguire (2001). 'Big Questions in Public Network Management Research'. *Journal of Public Administration Research and Theory* **11** (July): 295–326.

Ainley, P. (2001). 'From a National System Locally Administered to a National System Nationally Administered: The New Leviathan in Education and Training in England'. *Journal of Social Policy* **30**(3): 457–476.

Astle, J. and C. Ryan, eds. (2008). *Academies and the future of state education.* London, CentreForum.

Axhausen, K. (2002). *A dynamic understanding of travel demand: A sketch.* ESRC Mobile Network Workshop, Cambridge.

Bache, I. (2003). 'Governing through Governance: Education Policy Control under New Labour'. *Political Studies* **51**(2): 300–314.

Ball, S.J. (1994). *Education reform: A critical and post-structural approach.* Buckingham, Open University Press.

Ball, S.J. (2003). 'The Teacher's Soul and the Terrors of Performativity.' *Journal of Education Policy* **18**(2): 215–228.

Ball, S.J. (2007). *Education plc: Understanding private sector participation in public sector education.* London, Routledge.

Ball, S.J. (2008a). 'New Philanthropy, New Networks and New Governance in Education'. *Political Studies* **56**(4): 747–765.

Ball, S.J. (2008b). *The education debate: Politics and policy in the 21st century.* Bristol, The Policy Press.

Ball, S.J. (2009). 'Privatising Education, Privatising Education Policy, Privatising Educational Research: Network Governance and the "Competition State"'. *Journal of Education Policy* **42**(1): 83–99.

Ball, S.J. (2010a). 'New Voices, New Knowledges and the New Politics of Education Research'. *European Educational Research Journal* **9**(2): 124–137.

Ball, S.J. (2010b). 'Social and Education Policy, Social Enterprise, Hybridity and New Discourse Communities'. Social Policy Association Conference. University of Lincoln.

Ball, S.J. (2010c). 'Is there a Global Middle Class? The Beginnings of a Cosmopolitan Sociology of Education: A Review'. *Journal of Comparative Education* **69**: 135–159.

Ball, S.J. (2011). 'Academies, Policy Networks and Governance.' In H. Gunter, ed. *The state and education policy: The academies programme*. London, Continuum: 146–158.

Ball, S.J. (2012). *Global Ed. Inc.: New policy networks and the neoliberal imaginary*. London, Routledge.

Ball, S.J. and S. Exley (2010). 'Making Policy with "Good Ideas": Policy Networks and the "Intellectuals" of New Labour'. *Journal of Education Policy* **25**(2): 151–169.

Bannock, C. (2003). *Evaluation of new ways of working in local education authorities*. Vol 1, Main Report, London, DfES.

Bartley, T. (2007). 'How Foundations Shape Social Movements: The Construction of an Organizational Field and the Rise of Forest Certification'. *Social Problems* **54**(3): 229–255.

Besussi, E. (2006). 'Mapping European Research Networks'. Working Papers Series No. 103. Retrieved 7 August 2009, from Mapping European Research Networks.

Bevir, M. and R.A.W. Rhodes (2003). 'Searching for Civil Society: Changing Patterns of Governance in Britain'. *Public Administration* **81**(1): 41–62.

Bevir, M. and R.A.W. Rhodes (2006). *Governance Stories*. London, Routledge.

Blackburn, R. (2006). 'Finance and the Fourth Dimension'. *New Left Review* **39** (May/June): 39–70.

Blair, T. (2005) Speech to parents introducing the Labour government's White Paper on secondary education, 24 August, Downing Street, London. Available: http://news.bbc.co.uk/1/hi/uk_politics/4372216.stm.

Blond, P. (2009). *The ownership state*. London, ResPublica.

Bochel, H., ed. (2011). *The Conservative Party and social policy*. Bristol, The Policy Press.

Börzel, T. (1997). 'What's so Special about Policy Networks? An Exploration of the Concept and Its Usefulness in Studying European Governance.' *European Integration Online Papers* 1 (016), available: http://eiop.or.at/eiop/texte/1997-016a.htm

Bourdieu, P. (1985). 'The social space and the genesis of groups'. *Theory and Society* **14**: 723–744.

Bourdieu, P. (2004). 'Forms of Capital'. In S.J. Ball, ed. *The RoutledgeFalmer Reader in the Sociology of Education*. London, RoutledgeFalmer: 15–29.

Brant, J. and A. Falk (2007). 'Enterprise Education: Teaching Enterprise or Enterprising Teachers?', *Learning for Life* **6**(March): 4.

Breeze, B. (2007). *More than money: Why should sociologists be interested in philanthropy*. British Sociological Association, University of East London.

Burch, P.E. (2009). *Hiddens markets: The new educational privatization*. New York, Routledge.

Burt, R. S. (2001). 'Structural Holes versus Network Closure as Social Capital. In N. Lin, K. Cook and R.S. Burt, eds. *Social capital: Theory and research*. New York, Aldine De Gruyter: 31–56.

Cabinet Office (2006). *The UK government's approach to public service reform*. Prime Minister's Strategy Unit, Public Service Reform Team.

Cabinet Office (2008). *Excellence and Fairness: Achieving world class public services*. London, Cabinet Office.

Cabinet Office (2010). *The Coalition: Our programme for government*. London, Cabinet Office.

Cabinet Office (2011a) *Open Public Services*. White Paper. Cm 8145. London, The Stationery Office.

Cabinet Office (2011b). *Growing the social investment market: A vision and strategy*. London, Cabinet Office.

Campbell, C., J. Evans, et al (2004). *Evaluation of Education Partnership Boards*. London, Institute of Education, University of London.

Castells, M. (2000a). 'Materials for an Exploratory Theory of the Network Society.' *British Journal of Sociology* 51(1): 5–24.

Castells, M. (2000b). *The rise of the network society. The information age: economy, society and culture. Volume 1*. Malden, Blackwell.

Castells, M. (2004). 'Power and Politics in the Network Society'. Ralph Miliband Memorial Lecture. London School of Economics and Political Science. 14 March. Available: http://arkkitehtuuri.tkk.fi/YKS/fin/opetus/kurssit/yks_teoria/luennot/Castells/Castells-LSE-lecture.pdf.

Christopoulos, D. C. (2008). 'The Governance of Networks: Heuristic or Formal Analysis? A Reply to Rachel Parker'. *Political Studies* 56(2): 475–481.

Clarke, J. and J. Newman (1997). *The managerial state*. London, Sage.

Clarke, J. and J. Newman (2009). *Publics, politics and power: Changing the public of public services*. London, Sage.

Cohen, N. (2004). *Pretty straight guys*. London, Faber and Faber.

Coleman, W.D. and G. Skogstad, eds. (1990). *Policy communities and public policy in Canada*. Toronto, Copp Clark Pitman.

Courpasson, D. and M. Reed (2004). 'Introduction: Bureacracry in the Age of Enterprise.' *Organization* 11(1): 5–12.

Crane, A., A. McWilliams et al, eds. (2009). *The Oxford handbook of corporate social responsibility*, Oxford Handbooks in Business and Management. Oxford, Oxford University Press.

Davies, J.S. (2002). 'The Governance of Urban Regeneration: A Critique of the "Governing without Government" Thesis'. *Public Administration* **80**(2): 301–322.

Davies, J.S. (2005). 'Local Governance and the Dialectics of Hierarchy, Market and Network.' *Policy Studies* **26**(3/4): 311–335.

Dean, M. (2007). *Governing societies: Political perspectives on domestic and international rule.* Maidenhead, Open University Press.

Department for Children Schools and Families (2008). *Back on track. A strategy for modernising alternative provision for young people.* White Paper. London, DCSF.

Department for Education (2010). *The importance of teaching.* The Schools White Paper 2010. Cm 7980, London. Department for Education.

DfES (Department for Education and Skills) (2003). *Raising standards and tackling workload: A national agreement.* Series Title *0172 2003.* Available: https://www.education.gov.uk/publications/eOrderingDownload/DfES%200172%20200MIG1975.pdf.

DfES (2004). *Five year strategy for children and learners.* Cm 6272. London, Department for Education and Skills.

Dicken, P., P.F. Kelly, et al (2001). 'Chains and Networks, Territories and Scales: towards a Relational Framework for Analysing the Global Economy.' *Global Networks* **1**(1): 89–112.

Dowding, K. (1995). 'Model or Metaphor: A Critical Review of the Network Approach'. *Political Studies* **43**(1): 136–158.

du Gay, P. (2004). 'Against "Enterprise" (but not against "Enterprise", for that Would Make no Sense).' *Organization* **11**(1): 37–57.

du Gay, P. (2008). 'Keyser Süze Elites: Market Populism and the Politics of Institutional Change.' *The Sociological Review* **56**(1): 80–102.

Eggers, W. (2008). 'The Changing Nature of Government: Network Governance.' In J. O'Flynn and J. Wanna, eds. *Collaborative governance: A new era of public policy in Australia?.* Canberra, ANU E Press: 23–28.

Ellison, N. (2011). 'The Conservative Party and the "Big Society"'. In C. Holden, M. Kilkey and G. Ramia, eds. *Social Policy Review 23: Analysis and debate in social policy.* Bristol, The Policy Press, 45–62.

Every Child a Chance Trust (2009). *The long term costs of numeracy difficulties.* Available: www.everychildachancetrust.org/downloads/ecc/Long%20term%20costs%20of%20numeracy%20difficulties.pdf.

Exley, S. and S.J. Ball (2011). 'Something Old, Something New: Understanding Conservative Education Policy'. In H. Bochel, ed. *The Conservative Party and social policy.* Bristol, The Policy Press. 97–118.

Fairclough, N. (2000). *New Labour, new language*. London, Routledge.

Finlayson, A. (2003). *Making sense of New Labour*. London, Lawrence and Wishart.

Finlayson, A. (2008). 'From Economic Revolution to Social Revolution: Oliver Letwin talks to Alan Finlayson.' *Soundings* **40**: 112–122.

Foucault, M. (1974). *The archaeology of knowledge*. London, Tavistock.

Fuller, A., L. Unwin, et al (2010). *Economic regeneration, social cohesion, and the welfare-to-work industry: Innovation, opportunity and compliance in the city-region*. London, LLAKES, Institute of Education.

Gibson, H. (2008). 'Ideology, Instrumentality and Economics Education: on the Secretion of Values within Philanthropy, Financial Capability and Enterprise Education in English Schools.' *International Review of Economics Education* **7**(2): 57–78.

Giddens, A. (1991). *Modernity and self-identity*. Cambridge, Polity.

Goodwin, M. (2009). 'Which Networks Matter in Educational Governance? A Reply to Ball's "New Philanthropy, New Networks and New Governance in Education".' *Political Studies* **57**(3): 608–687.

Gordon, C. (1991). 'Governmental Rationality: an Introduction'. In G. Burchell, C. Gordon and P. Miller, eds. *The Foucault effect: Studies in governmentality*. Brighton, Harvester/Wheatsheaf: 1–51.

Grabher, G. (2004). 'Learning in Projects, Remembering in Networks? Communality, Sociality, and Connectivity in Project Ecologies'. *European Urban and Regional Studies* **11**(2): 103–123.

Granovetter, M. (1973). 'The Strength of Weak Ties.' *American Journal of Sociology* **78**: 1360–1380.

Granovetter, M. (1985). 'Economic Action and Social Structure: The Problem of Embeddedness.' *American Journal of Sociology* **91**(3): 481–510.

Greenaway, J., B. Salter, et al (2007). 'How Policy Networks can Damage Democratic Health: A Case Study in the Government of Governance'. *Public Administration* **85**(3): 717–738.

Grimaldi, E. (2011). 'Governance and Heterarchy in Education: Enacting Networks for School Innovation.' *Italian Journal of Sociology of Education* **2**(1): 114–149.

Gunter, H., ed. (2010). *The state and education policy: The academies programme*. London, Continuum.

Handy, C. (2006). *The new philanthropists: The new generosity*. London, William Heinemann.

Harrison, S. and B. Wood (1999). 'Designing Health Service Organisation in the UK, 1968–98: From Blueprint to Bright Idea and "Manipulated Emergence".' *Public Administration* **77**(4): 751–768.

Harvey, C. and M. Maclean (2008). 'Capital Theory and the Dynamics of Elite Business Networks in Britain and France.' *The Sociological Review* **56**(Issue Supplement s1): 103–120.

Hatcher, R. (2011). 'Liberating the Supply Side, Managing the Market'. In R. Hatcher and K. Jones, eds. *No country for the young: Education from New Labour to the Coalition*. London, Tufnell Press: 18–36.

Hatcher, R. (2012). 'Democracy and Governance in the Local School System.' *Journal of Education Administration and History* (forthcoming).

Hodge, G.A. and K. Coghill (2007). 'Accountability in the Privatized State'. *Governance* **20**: 675–702.

Holmgren, C. and J. From (2005). 'Taylorism of the Mind: Entrepreneurship Education from a Perspective of Educational Research'. *European Educational Research Journal* **4**(4): 382–390.

Hood, C. (1990). *Beyond the public bureaucracy state: Public administration in the 1990s*. London, LSE.

Howard, P.N. (2002). 'Network Ethnography and the Hyermedia Organization: New Media, New Organizations, New Methods'. *New Media and Society*, **4**(4): 550–574.

Jessop, B. (1994). 'The Transition to post-Fordism and the Schumpeterian Workfare State'. In R. Burrows and B. Loader, eds. *Towards a post-Fordist welfare state?*. London, Routledge: 13–37.

Jessop, B. (1997). 'The Entrepreneurial City: Re-imagining Localities, Redesigning Economic Governance, or Restructuring Capital?'. In N. Jewson and S. Macgregor, eds. *Transforming cities: Contested governance and spatial dimensions*. London, Routledge: 28–41.

Jessop, B. (1998). 'The Rise of Governance and the Risks of Failure'. *International Social Science Journal* **155**(1): 29–45.

Jessop, B. (2002). *The future of the capitalist state*. Cambridge, Polity.

Jones, K. (2003). *Education in Britain: 1944 to the present*. Cambridge, Polity Press.

Keast, R., Mandell, M. and Brown, K. (2006). 'Mixing state, market and network governance modes: the role of government in "crowded" policy domains'. *Journal of Organizational Theory and Behaviour*, **1**(19): 27–50.

Kickert, W.J.M., E.H. Klijn, et al (1997). 'Managing Networks in the Public Sector: Findings and Reflections'. In W.J.M. Kickert, E.H. Klijn and J.F.M. Koppenjan, eds. *Managing complex networks: Strategies for the public sector*. Thousand Oaks, CA, Sage: 166–191.

Kingdon, J.W. (1995). *Agendas, alternatives, and public policies*. New York, HarperCollins.

Kisby, B. (2010). 'The Big Society: Power to the People?'. *The Political Quarterly* **81**(4): 484–491.

Knox, H., M. Savage, et al (2006). 'Social Networks and the Study of Relations: Networks as Method, Metaphor and Form'. *Economy and Society* **35**(1): 113–140.

Kooiman, J., ed. (1993). *Modern governance: New government–society interactions*. London, Sage.

Kooiman, J. (2003). *Governing as governance*. London, Sage.

Koppenjan, J. and Klijn, E.-H. (2004). *Managing uncertainties in networks: Public private controversies*. London, Routledge.

Larner, W. (2003). 'Neoliberalism?'. *Environment and Planning D: Society and Space* **21**: 509–512.

Larner, W. and M. Butler (2005). '"Governmentalities of Local Partnerships": the Rise of a Partnering State in New Zealand'. *Studies in Political Economy* **75**: 85–108.

Lemke, T. (2001). '"The Birth of Bio-politics" – Michel Foucault's Lecture at the College de France on Neoliberal Governmentality'. *Economy and Society* **30**(2): 190–207.

Lin, N. (2002). *Social capital: A theory of social structure and action*. Cambridge, Cambridge University Press.

Ling, T. (2000). 'Unpacking Partnership: The Case of Health Care.' In D. Clarke, S. Gewirtz and E. McLaughlin, eds. *New Managerialism, New Welfare?*. London, Sage: 82–101.

Lister, J. (2011). *Corporate social responsibility and the state. International approaches to forest co-regulation*. Vancouver–Toronto, UBC Press.

Loughlin, J. (2004). 'The "Transformation" of Governance: New Directions in Social Policy'. *Australian Journal of Politics and History* **50**(1): 8–22.

Lubienski, C. (2009). *Do quasi-markets foster innovation in education? A comparative perspective*. Education Working Paper No. 25. Paris, OECD.

McCann, E.J. (2011). 'Urban Policy Mobilities and Global Circuits of Knowledge: Toward a research agenda'. *Annals of the Association of American Geographers* **101**(1): 107–130.

McCormick, R., A. Fox, et al (2011). *Researching and understanding educational networks*. London, Routledge.

Mackenzie, R. and M. M. Lucio (2005). 'The Realities of Regulatory Change: Beyond the Fetish of Deregulation'. *British Journal of Sociology* **39**(3): 499–517.

MacKinnon, D. (2000). 'Managerialism, Governmentality and the State: a Neo-Foucauldian Approach to Local Economic Governance'. *Political Geography* **19**(3): 293–314.

McPherson, A. and C. Raab (1988). *Governing education: A sociology of policy since 1945*. Edinburgh, Edinburgh University Press.

Maile, S. and P. Hoggett (2001). 'Best Value and the Politics of Pragmatism'. *Policy and Politics* **29**(4): 509–516.

March, J.G. and J.P. Olsen (1989). *Rediscovering institutions: The organisational basis of politics.* New York, Free Press.

Marin, B. and R. Mayntz, eds. (1991). *Policy networks: Empirical evidence and theoretical considerations.* Frankfurt am Main, Campus Verlag; Boulder, CO, Westview.

Marinetto, M. (2003). 'Governing beyond the Centre: A Critique of the Anglo-Governance School'. *Political Studies* **51**(3): 592–608.

Marsh, D. and R. Rhodes, eds. (1992). *Policy networks in British government.* Oxford, Clarendon Press.

Marsh, D. and M. Smith (2000). 'Understanding Policy Networks: towards a Dialectical Approach.' *Political Studies* **48**: 4–21.

Marshall, P., J. Moses, et al (2006). *Aiming higher: A better future for England's schools.* London, CentreForum.

Martin, S. and Y. Muschamp (2008). 'Education: from the Comprehensive to the Individual.' In M. Powell, ed. *Modernising the welfare state: The Blair legacy.*. Bristol, The Policy Press: 91–104.

May, J., P. Cloke, et al (2005). 'Re-phasing Neoliberalism: New Labour and Britain's Crisis of Street Homelessness'. *Antipode* **37**(4): 704–730.

Mintrom, M. and S. Vergari (1996). 'Advocacy Coalitions, Policy Entrepreneurs, and Policy Change'. *Policy Studies Journal* **24**(3): 420–434.

Miron, G., J.L. Urschel and N. Saxton (2011) *What Makes KIPP Work? A Study of Student Characteristics, Attrition, and School Finance.* National Center for the Study of Privatization in Education, Teachers College, Columbia University and Study Group on Educational Management Organizations at Western Michigan University. Available at www. edweek.org/media/kippstudy.pdf

Mok, K.H. (2007). 'Globalisation, New Education Governance and State Capacity in East Asia'. *Globalisation, Societies and Education* **5**(1): 1–21.

Monahan, T. (2005). *Globalization, technological change, and public education.* New York, Routledge.

Moore, S.E.H. (2008). *Ribbon culture: Charity, compassion and public awareness.* Basingstoke, Palgrave Macmillan.

Newman, J. (2001). *Modernising governance: New Labour, policy and society.* London, Sage.

Oborn, E., M. Barrett, et al (2011). 'Policy Entrepreneurship in the Development of Public Sector Strategy: the Case of London Health Reform'. *Public Administration* **89**(2): 325–344.

Osborne, D. and T. Gaebler (1992). *Re-inventing government*. Reading, MA, Addison-Wesley.

Ozga, J. (2008). 'Governing Knowledge: Research steering and research quality'. *European Educational Research Journal* **7**(3): 261-272.

Pal, L. A. (1997) 'Virtual Policy Networks: The Internet as a Model of Contemporary Governance?'. *Proceedings of ISOC*. Available: www.isoc.org/inet97/proceedings/G7/G7_1.htm.

Parker, R. (2007). 'Networked Governance or Just Networks? Local Governance of the Knowledge Economy in Limerick (Ireland) and Karlskrona (Sweden)'. *Political Studies* **55**(1): 113–132.

Peck, J. (2003). 'Geography and Public Policy: Mapping the Penal State'. *Progress in Human Geography* **27**(2): 222–232.

Peck, J. (2004) 'Geography and Public Policy: Constructions of Neoliberalism'. *Progress in Human Geography* **28**: 392-405.

Peterson, J. (2003). *Policy networks*. Vienna, Institute for Advanced Studies.

Pierre, J., ed. (2000). *Debating governance*. Oxford, Oxford University Press.

Pierre, J. and B.G. Peters (2000). *Governance, politics, and the state*. Basingstoke, Macmillan Press.

Pollack, A. (2004). *NHS plc: The privatisation of our health care*. London, Verso.

Powell, J.L. and M. Edwards (2005). 'Surveillance and Morality: Revisiting the Education Reform Act (1988) in the United Kingdom'. *Surveillance & Society* **3**(1): 96–106.

Provan, K.G. and P. Kenis (2008). 'Modes of Network Governance: Structure, Management, and Effectiveness'. *Journal of Public Administration Research and Theory* **18**(2): 229–252.

Rabinow, P. (2003). *Anthropos today: Reflections on modern equipment*. Princeton, Princeton University Press.

Reckhow, S. (2010). 'Disseminating and Legitimating a new approach: the role of foundations'. In K.E. Bulkley, J.R. Henig and H.M. Levin, eds. *Between public and private: Politics, governance and the new portfolio models of urban school reform*. Cambridge, MA, Harvard Education Press.

Rendtorff, J. (2008). *Corporate citizenship, trust and accountability*. Department of Communication, Business and Information Technology, Roskilde University.

Rhodes, R. (1995). *The new governance: Governing without government*. State of Britain ESRC/RSA Seminar Series. Swindon, ESRC.

Rhodes, R.A.W. (1981). *Control and power in central–local relations*. Aldershot, Gower.

Rhodes, R.A.W. (1988). 'Policy networks, territorial communities and British government'. Paper presented to the Workshop on Public Policy in Northern Ireland: Adoption or Adaptation, Policy Research Institute. University of Ulster, 4 March 1988.

Rhodes, R.A.W. (1996). 'The New Governance: Governing without Government'. *Political Studies* **54**: 652–667.

Rhodes, R.A.W. (1997). *Understanding governance: Policy networks, governance, reflexivity and accountability.* Buckingham, Open University Press.

Richards, D. and M.J. Smith (2002). *Governance and public policy in the United Kingdom.* Oxford, Oxford University Press.

Riles, A. (2000). *The network inside out.* Ann Arbor, University of Michigan Press.

Roberts, J. (2003). 'The Manufacture of Corporate Social Responsibility: Constructing Corporate Sensibility'. *Organization* **10**(2): 249–265.

Rose, N. (1999). *Powers of freedom: Reframing political thought.* Cambridge, Cambridge University Press.

Rose, N. (2000). 'Government and Control'. In D. Garland and R. Sparks, eds. *Criminology and social theory.* New York, Oxford University Press: 183–208.

Rose, N. (2007). 'Psychology as a Social Science'. Retrieved 2 June 2010. Available: www.lse.ac.uk/collections/socialPsychology/pdf/Psychology%20as%20a%20Social%20Science%20-%20LSE%20-%20February%2007.pdf.

Sanghera, B. (2011). 'Charitable Giving, Everyday Morality and a Critique of Bourdieusian Theory: An Investigation into Disinterested Judgements, Moral Concerns and Reflexivity in the UK'. Working paper, School of Social Policy, Sociology and Social Research, University of Kent.

Savage, M. and K. Williams, eds. (2008). *Remembering elites.* Oxford, Blackwell.

Sbragia, A. (2002). 'Governance, the State, and the Market: What is Going On?'. *Governance* **13**(2): 243–250.

Scharpf, F.W. (1994). 'Games Real Actors Could Play: Positive and Negative Coordination in Embedded Organisations'. *Journal of Theoretical Politics* **6**(1): 27–53.

Scharpf, F.W. (1997). *Games real actors play: Actor-centered institutionalism in policy research.* Oxford, West View Point.

Shamir, R. (2008). 'The Age of Responsibilitization: on Market-embedded Morality'. *Economy and Society* **37**(1): 1–19.

Singh, A.K. and R. Stevens (2007). *From networking: Towards a better tomorrow*. New Delhi, India, South Asian Network for Social and Agricultural Development.

Sison, A. (2003). *The moral capital of leaders: Why virtue matters*. Cambridge, MA, Edward Elgar.

Skelcher, C. (1998). *The appointed state*. Buckingham, Open University Press.

Skelcher, C. (2000). 'Changing Images of the State – Overloaded, Hollowed-out, Congested'. *Public Policy and Administration* **15**(3): 3–19.

Skelcher, C. (2007). 'Democracy in Collaborative Spaces: Why Context Matters in Researching Governance Networks.' In M. Marcussen and J. Torfing, eds. *Democratic network governance in Europe*. Basingstoke, Palgrave Macmillan: 25–46.

Skelcher, C., N. Mathur, et al (2004). *Negotiating the institutional void: Discursive aligments, collaborative institutions and democratic governance*. Institute of Local Government Studies, University of Birmingham.

Skogstad, G. (2005). 'Policy Networks and Policy Communities: Conceptual Evolution and Governing Realities'. Workshop on Canada's Contribution to Comparative Theorizing, Canadian Political Science Association, University of Western Ontario.

Smith, A. (2000). 'Policy Networks and Advocacy Coalitions: Explaining Policy Change and Continuity in UK Industrial Pollution Policy?'. *Environment and Planning C: Government and Policy* **18**: 95–114.

Smith, M. (2010). 'From Big Government to Big Society: Changing The State–Society Balance'. *Parliamentary Affairs* **63**(4): 818–833.

Sørensen, E. and J. Torfing, eds. (2008). *Theories of democratic network governance*. Basingstoke, Palgrave

Stevenson, H., B. Carter, et al (2007) '"New Professionalism", Workforce Remodeling and the Restructuring of Teachers' Work'. *International Electronic Journal for Leadership and Learning* **11**(18). Available: www.ucalgary.ca/iejll/.

Stoker, G. (1998). 'Governance as Theory: Five Propositions'. **50**(155): 17–28.

Stoker, G. (2004). *Transforming local governance: From Thatcherism to New Labour*. Basingstoke, Palgrave.

Sukarieh, M. and S. Tannock (2009). 'Putting School Commercialism in Context: A Global History of Junior Achievement Worldwide'. *Journal of Education Policy* **24**(6): 769–786.

Sullivan, H. (2003). 'New Forms of Local Accountability: Coming to terms with "many hands"?'. *Policy & Politics* **31**(3): 353-369.

Sullivan, H. and C. Skelcher (2004). *Working across boundaries: Collaboration in public services (government beyond the centre).* Basingstoke, Palgrave Macmillan.

Taylor, A. (2000). 'Hollowing Out or Filling In? Taskforces and the Management of Cross-cutting Issues in British Government'. *The British Journal of Politics & International Relations* **2**(1): 46–71.

Teisman, G.R. and E.H. Klijn (2002). 'Partnership Arrangements: Governmental Rhetoric or Governance Scheme?'. *Public Administration Review* **62**(2): 197–205.

Thaler, R. and C. Sunstein (2008). *Nudge: Improving decisions about health, wealth, and happiness.* New Haven and London, Yale University Press.

Thrift, N. (2005). *Knowing capitalism.* London, Sage.

Tickell, A. and J. Peck (2002). 'Neoliberalizing Space'. *Antipode* **34**(3): 380–404.

Tickly, L. (2003). 'Postcolonialism and Comparative Education'. *International Review of Education* **23**(1): 97–112.

Tomlinson, S. (2001). *Education in a post-welfare society.* Buckingham, Open University Press.

Triantafillou, P. (2004a). 'Addressing Network Governance through the Concepts of Governmentality and Normalization'. *Administrative Theory & Praxis* **26**: 489–508.

Triantafillou, P. (2004b). *Conceiving 'network governance': The potential of the concepts of governmentality and normalization.* Working Paper 4, Roskilde, Denmark, Centre for Democratic Network Governance.

Urry, J. (2003). 'Social Networks, Travel and Talk'. *British Journal of Sociology* **54**(2): 155–175.

Urry, J. (2004). 'Small Worlds and the New "Social Physics"'. *Global Networks* **4**(2): 109–130.

Urry, J. (2010). 'Mobile Sociology'. *The British Journal of Sociology – The BJS: Shaping Sociology over 60 years*: 347–366.

Walker, D. (2007). 'Power of Three'. *RSA Journal* **February**: 56–59.

Wanna, J. (2009). 'Political Chronicles, Commonwealth of Australia July to December 2008'. *Australian Journal of Politics and History* **55**(2): 261–315.

Watts, D.J. (1999). 'Networks, Dynamics and the Small World Phenomenon'. *American Journal of Sociology* **105**(2): 493–527.

Webb, A. (1991). 'Co-ordination: A Problem in Public Sector Management'. *Policy and Politics* **19**(4): 229–241.

Whatmore, S. and L. Thorne (1997). 'Nourishing Networks: Alternative Geographies of Food'. In D. Goodman and M. Watts, eds. *Globalising food: Agrarian questions and global restructuring.* New York, Routledge: 287–304.

Whitehead, M. (2003). '"In the Shadow of Hierarchy": Meta-governance, Policy Reform and Urban Regeneration in the West Midlands'. *AREA* **35**(1): 6–14.

Whitty, G. (2006). *Teacher professionalism in a new era*. First General Teaching Council for Northern Ireland Annual Lecture, Belfast.

Williams, P. (2002). 'The competent boundary spanner.' *Public Administration,* **80**(1): 103–124.

Wilson, D. (2003). 'Unravelling Control Freakery: Redefining Central–Local Government Relations'. *British Journal of Politics and International Relations* **5**(3): 317–346.

Wolch, J. (1990). *The shadow state: Government and voluntary sector in transition*. New York, The Foundation Center.

Woods, P.A., G.J. Woods, et al (2007). 'Academies Schools: Sponsors, Specialisms and Varieties of Entrepreneurial Leadership'. *Journal of Education Policy* **22**(2): 263–285.

Wright-Mills, C. (1959). *The power elite*. New York, Oxford University Press.

Index

Note: Page numbers in *italics* refer to figures, tables and boxes. Page numbers followed by the letter *n*, e.g. 17*n*, refer to footnotes. Page numbers in **bold** refer to major treatment of a topic. Page numbers followed by App refer to the appendix.